T0328572

Cambridge Elements ☰

Elements in the Problems of God
edited by
Michael L. Peterson
Asbury Theological Seminary

EVIL AND THEODICY

Laura W. Ekstrom
William & Mary

CAMBRIDGE
UNIVERSITY PRESS

Shaftesbury Road, Cambridge CB2 8EA, United Kingdom

One Liberty Plaza, 20th Floor, New York, NY 10006, USA

477 Williamstown Road, Port Melbourne, VIC 3207, Australia

314–321, 3rd Floor, Plot 3, Splendor Forum, Jasola District Centre, New Delhi – 110025, India

103 Penang Road, #05–06/07, Visioncrest Commercial, Singapore 238467

Cambridge University Press is part of Cambridge University Press & Assessment, a department of the University of Cambridge.

We share the University's mission to contribute to society through the pursuit of education, learning and research at the highest international levels of excellence.

www.cambridge.org
Information on this title: www.cambridge.org/9781009293044

DOI: 10.1017/9781009293075

First published 2023

A catalogue record for this publication is available from the British Library.

ISBN 978-1-009-29304-4 Paperback
ISSN 2754-8724 (online)
ISSN 2754-8716 (print)

Evil and Theodicy

Elements in the Problems of God

DOI: 10.1017/9781009293075
First published online: January 2023

Laura W. Ekstrom
William & Mary

Author for correspondence: Laura W. Ekstrom, lwekst@wm.edu

Abstract: Suffering is ubiquitous. Quests to make sense of it in relation to the existence of God – and to find meaning in our lives in the face of it – are significant aspects of the human experience. *Evil and Theodicy* motivates the project of theodicy by examining arguments rooted in evil against God's existence and by critically assessing the response of skeptical theism. Ekstrom explores eight different lines of theodicy. She argues that, even if the prospects for theodicy are dim with respect to defending the rationality of theistic belief in light of suffering, nonetheless, work in theodicies is practically useful.

Keywords: pointless evil, free will, suffering, God, theodicy

ISBNs: 9781009293044 (PB), 9781009293075 (OC)
ISSNs: 2754-8724 (online), 2754-8716 (print)

Contents

1 God, Evil, and Justification

It is not pleasant to turn one's gaze toward the suffering experienced in life, but it is inescapable. Inevitably we endure heartbreak and physical pain in our personal lives, and we confront our own vulnerability to injury and disease, as well to disrespect and mistreatment, to betrayal, to loss, and to premature death. Beyond our individual minds and bodies, the losses and pains that come to those we love – our sons and daughters, our partners, our brothers and sisters, our closest friends – may cut even more deeply. We hurt when they hurt, and it is deeply vexing to attempt to understand why they could possibly be made to endure the setbacks, the injuries, the diseases, and the injustices they do. To widen our view to the suffering of our fellow human inhabitants of the globe at the current moment, we need only – and we should – read and listen to documentary filmmakers and journalists' reports: a pregnant woman whose pelvis is shattered in a bombing in Ukraine and the millions of Ukrainian mothers, fathers, and children who have lost everything in a senseless invasion; an Indian heat wave causing deaths from dehydration among people living in poverty in homes lacking insulation and cooling systems; innocent people going about their shopping in the United States, shot to death in a rampage by a racist gunman in the grip of a white nationalist "replacement" conspiracy theory; the ungraspable numbers in the millions of those who have died – and those who remain alive, in deep grief over losing those who have died – in an ongoing global COVID-19 pandemic.

We look backward to history and see scenes of grotesque violence and cruelty. Use of terms such as the transatlantic slave trade, the Holocaust, the Rwandan genocide can seem wrong in virtue of their generalness. Labels can obscure – and keep us feeling psychologically safe, in a way that should be challenged – the individual realities of what was experienced and endured in historical atrocities: female enslaved persons forced to bear the children of slave owners only to have their infants stolen from them at birth to be sold and used, never seen again by their mothers; the slow, wasting, painful death of starvation through forced hard labor in prison camps; the brutality inflicted in beheadings by machetes in front of family members; Native American children forced into assimilation "schools," subjected to cultural erasure as well as emotional and physical abuse; malicious murders motivated by hatred for people because of their sexual orientation; countless maternal deaths in the natural process of childbirth, every one of them tragic.[1] We have not yet mentioned the nonhuman animal suffering that

---

[1] As reported in Kristoff and WuDunn (2009, pp. 98–99), the highest lifetime risk of dying in the process of childbirth is in Niger, where a woman or girl has a 1 in 7 chance of dying. Overall, in sub-Saharan Africa, the lifetime risk of dying in childbirth is 1 in 22. A woman in India has a 1 in 70 chance of dying in childbirth at some time in her life, compared to the United States, where the lifetime risk is 1 in 4,800, Italy, where it is 1 in 26,000, and Ireland, where it is (only) 1 in 47,600.

has occurred, and continues to occur, in the natural world, in the abuse of pets and in animal fights, and in heartless practices in factory farming.

Fixing our attention on the evils in our world can be so disheartening that it is not only diversions such as watching a comedy series or gardening that tempt us away, but anything at all distracting, even attending to bills, scrubbing messes, or doing the laundry. It takes courage to face the saddest and most devastating facts about the experience of life, for human beings and other sentient creatures. We need even more courage to sustain reflection on these facts with respect to their theological and metaphysical implications. These are not easy topics to work out, either emotionally or rationally.

Still, none of us can escape the painful and brutal aspects of human life. And billions of us do currently, or have in the past, believed in the existence of God. By 'God' we mean in this Element an absolutely perfect divine being, one who essentially is omniscient, omnipotent, and perfectly good and who is (if existent) Creator of the universe. Most of us at one point or another have wondered about how the world could contain the suffering it does if there were a God. How should one think about the question of the theoretical fit between a metaphysical picture of the world as created and overseen by God, on the one hand, and the realities of the atrocities and suffering we observe?

1.1 Defining Evil

Sometimes the word 'evil' is construed in such a way that it suggests malicious intent. On this understanding of the term, the suffering and devastation experienced during natural disasters, such as the destruction of possessions and lives in tsunamis, tornadoes, and pandemics, would not ordinarily be thought of as evils. They would not be construed as evils, that is, unless one were to think of such suffering and loss as sent to victims by some kind of supernatural agent out of maliciousness, so that the victims were *made victims on purpose*. Some philosophical treatments of theoretical problems concerning God and evil do suggest the possibility that all instances of suffering on Earth are brought about intentionally by agents. For instance, in Alvin Plantinga's (1974) highly influential theistic defense against an atheist's charge that theists have logically contradictory beliefs in believing, at the same time, that God exists and that the evils in our world exist, we find the suggestion that perhaps human and animal suffering at the hands of natural forces, such as hurricanes, lightning strikes, and viral scourges, is ultimately the result of

---

In more recent statistics provided by the World Health Organization, a woman's lifetime risk of maternal death, defined as the probability that a fifteen-year-old woman will eventually die of a maternal cause, including severe bleeding (mostly bleeding after childbirth), infection (usually after childbirth), and complications from delivery, is 1 in 5,400 in high-income countries and 1 in 45 in low-income countries (World Health Organization, 2019).

the bad free choices of beings we can't directly see. The suggestion is not that perhaps these instances of suffering are caused directly by the absolutely perfect being, God, but rather that, possibly, they are caused by created nonhuman beings who misuse their God-given power of free will to wreak havoc on Earth, beings such as spirits or demons. On this construal, "moral evils" are brought about intentionally by human agents, such as robbery at gunpoint, and "broadly moral evils" (what are more typically called "natural evils"), such as the destruction of homes and lives in floods, are (possibly) intentionally brought about by nonhuman (supernatural) agents.

Not all theists make appeal to such a possibility in their thinking about suffering in relation to God, and not all philosophers and theologians who address the "problem of evil" – or, rather, the cluster or family of perplexities and arguments pertaining to God's existence in light of the suffering we observe and experience – use the term 'evil' in the narrow sense that requires agency or malicious intent. In the philosophy of religion, the term 'evil' typically is used more broadly, to refer to any painful, rotten, wrong, distressing, or horrid aspect of life in our world, including our human vulnerability to emotional suffering, physical pain, injustice, torment, betrayal, loss, cruelty, injury, ruination, disease, and premature death. On this broader construal, the various forms of cancer count as evils, including childhood leukemia and osteosarcoma, as do inherited genetic diseases that result in disabilities and premature death, along with smallpox outbreaks, the 1918 flu pandemic, and the COVID-19 pandemic, even if we think of these (as most of us do) as unintended and the fault of no created agent at all.

1.2 An Argument from Pointless Evil

With this broad understanding of evil in place, we can begin to examine carefully the matter of why the reality of evil may be thought to pose a challenge to the rationality of belief in God. Our concern may focus on the bare existence of any evil at all, or it might focus on various facts about the evils we experience and observe in our world, such as how extremely intense they can be – painful to the limits of human endurance, and even exceeding those limits, causing death – and how widespread they are – afflicting sentient creatures across the globe and throughout history – and how they seem to be distributed in ways that appear unfair and inexplicable. Some people who are kind, good, and loving suffer from debilitating injuries, upon which are piled injustices, loneliness, and further afflictions, and then even more emotional, professional, physical, and social losses. Others who are self-centered, cruel or destructive live rather charmed lives with respect to material wealth and physical well-being. Certain cases of evil might strike us as so horrific that we cannot see any way it could make sense rationally to believe that God is really there, as Creator and sustainer of the universe, in light of them.

God – described by St. Anselm as *the being than which none greater can be conceived* – has as essential attributes every great-making quality, including omniscience, omnipotence, and perfect goodness. To have knowledge of some truths is a positively valuable trait, one that is limited in comparison to having knowledge of all truths and having no beliefs that are mistaken. God, as an essentially omniscient being, knows all the truths there are to be known and believes no falsehoods. This means that there is no pain or hardship that "escapes God's notice" or is outside God's realm of perception, unlike much of the suffering of others with respect to us, which happens without our awareness: in private, unshared with us, or across the world in some place we have never been or even heard of. Unlike us, God would not be ignorant about anyone's suffering – God would see and know of it all. Further, if God is perfectly good, then God would not want us to suffer. Insofar as we are good people, we do not want those we love and care about to suffer, and God, as our perfectly good Creator, would not be indifferent to our well-being, but would care about us. In addition, to have the power to do things is a positively valuable quality. God, as an essentially omnipotent being, has the power to do everything that can be done. If God is perfectly powerful, then God can eliminate any suffering he knows about and wants to eliminate. Here we have the basic line of reasoning in favor of the conclusion that, if God were to exist, then there would be no evil in the world. The argument is that God, as perfectly good, would not want us to suffer; and as perfectly knowing, God knows about all suffering; and as perfectly powerful, God can prevent all suffering. But there is suffering in the world. Thus, there is no God.

Here is a line of response to the argument in the previous paragraph. Sometimes, even if we are good people, we allow, or even cause, someone we care about to suffer, even though we could have prevented it, because we have their greater good in mind. A simple example is a good parent who takes her child to the physician's office to receive the vaccine for measles, mumps, and rubella. The child is distressed; the situation produces anxiety; and the injection hurts. Although the parent knows about the distress and pain, in taking the child to the physician and allowing the vaccination to be administered, she is not thereby a morally bad person. Why? Because the vaccination is known to help prevent the child from contracting a contagious disease. This observation suggests that it is perhaps mistaken to think that God would want us never to suffer at all. God might want us to suffer for some good reason known to God, making God's allowance, or even causation, of our suffering justifiable. This suggests that the perfect goodness of God implies that God would not want us to suffer when that suffering was *not needed* to bring about a greater good, which could include preventing an evil as bad or worse.

The question arises, of course, of why any suffering would be needed by God in order for God to bring about a greater good. How could it be that an omnipotent being would *need* anything at all in order to produce a desired outcome? God would not be constrained by what is physically necessary for bringing about some end, since God, if existent, is the Creator of the physical world and the laws of nature that govern its operation. Taking our children to be vaccinated against polio, measles, mumps, rubella, tuberculosis, tetanus, and other infectious diseases is not strictly causally necessary for preventing their acquiring one of these diseases – our children might very luckily avoid getting the disease, even though unvaccinated – and it is not causally sufficient for their not getting one of these diseases – they might get vaccinated, but then very unluckily get the disease anyway. But still, we are aware, based on ample evidence, that taking our children for these vaccinations and allowing them to endure the temporary distress and pain they bring is causally necessary for greatly lowering the odds that they will acquire one of these diseases, given that they exist in our world and given the ways they spread among people and the regularity of the laws of nature. We are not in charge of what infectious microorganisms there are in our world or in charge of how the natural world works. So we have to make compromises, so to speak, with respect to causing and allowing pain, given the realities in which we find ourselves, in order to do our best to promote the full well-being and flourishing of those we love. But God, as Creator and sustainer of the universe, is in charge of what exists – including which diseases exist – and how our world works – including the law of gravity, for instance, and how viruses and bacteria are transmitted, and how infectious microorganisms affect sentient creatures, and how our immune systems and our nervous systems work.

So God would not be bound by the natural laws that govern our world. God might, for instance, part the Red Sea or turn water to wine if so desired, and God could create worlds different from ours in which things work very differently from the ways they work in our world. Nonetheless, a theist may suggest, there might be logical necessities that govern the acquisition or realization of some goods that are of sufficiently high value and are such that not even God could realize those goods without causing or allowing some suffering to befall created beings. And if this were so, then God's perfect goodness could be upheld even in light of there being suffering on the part of created beings in our world. The logical impossibility of God's realizing the goods without the suffering would be akin to the logical impossibility of God's making a circular square: since there's no such thing to be done, it is no knock against God's omnipotence that God cannot do this nonthing. And perhaps God's perfect goodness could be upheld even in light of there being the horrifically intense instances of suffering there are, and the vast amount of suffering there is, and the distribution of suffering among different persons and sentient creatures that there is, if such facts (or facts equivalent to them in negative value) are logically necessary for the realization of the sufficiently greater goods.

It stands to reason, thus, that if God exists, then God has *justifying reasons* for causing or permitting the instances of suffering that occur in our world in that they are logically necessary for the realization of greater goods, where the greater good could itself be a vastly increased chance of the realization of certain goods. God would not cause or allow suffering *pointlessly*. A pointless evil is one for which there is no God-justifying reason for causing or allowing it to occur.

Over the course of more than three decades, William Rowe advanced arguments for the nonexistence of God rooted in instances of horrible evil regarding which there appear to be no reasons that could justify God in remaining inert while they occur. The argument from pointless evil, which derives from the work of Rowe (1979, 1988, 1996), especially his 1979 work, "The Problem of Evil and Some Varieties of Atheism," and is insightfully probed by Graham Oppy (2013) and Daniel Speak (2015), among others, is as follows.

Argument from Pointless Evil:

   (1) If God exists, then our world does not contain any instances of pointless evil.
   (2) Our world contains an instance (or instances) of pointless evil.
   (3) Therefore, God does not exist.

In the subsequent sections, I will take up, in turn, each of the two premises of this argument, offering support for the first and second premises and critically examining some replies.

1.3 Support for Premise 1 of the Argument from Pointless Evil

I have roughly indicated in Section 1.2 the line of reasoning that leads up to the first premise of the argument from pointless evil. Here is further support. When we nondivine human agents intentionally cause or allow harm to others, we sometimes do so out of maliciousness, and we sometimes do so not maliciously but because we think there is no other or better way of bringing about a greater good for the one we hurt. In addition to arranging for vaccinations, we also, for instance, enforce consequences for bad behavior that temporarily grieve our children. When we fail to act to prevent the suffering of others, this is sometimes from a lack of knowledge – we were unaware of the abuse being suffered by the child in our neighborhood – and it is sometimes due to a lack of power – we cannot feed all those who are starving to death, and we may find that we cannot intervene in a crime without harming ourselves. But none of the excuses for failing to help that apply to us, as beings who are limited in knowledge and power, would apply to an absolutely perfect being who has all knowledge and power: God cannot be harmed and can do everything there is to be done, and no instance of suffering would escape God's notice. Further, as an essentially good being, God would not act maliciously. Hence there is good reason for thinking that, if God exists – since God is essentially omnipotent, omniscient, and perfectly good – everything that happens in the world involving suffering must be something that God causes or allows for some justifying reason. If God were to exist, then there would have to be some justifying reasons for which God causes or allows each instance of suffering in our world to occur, or else that suffering would be something God did not know about or failed to notice – which is impossible, given that God is all-knowing – or that suffering was something God did not care about or which God knew to be unnecessary for bringing about a greater good – which is impossible, given that God is perfectly good – or that suffering was something God had no power over whatsoever – which is impossible, given that God is omnipotent. Therefore, if God exists, then our world does not contain any instances of pointless evil.

Let me put the case for the truth of Premise 1 even more carefully, in a way that might head off some potential misunderstandings and objections. (This is how I express the supporting argument in Ekstrom [2021, p. 16].) Since God is essentially omniscient, God knows all truths there are to be known, including all truths about the instances of evil that occur in our world. If God is said not to know *ahead of time* that certain evils occur – owing to, for instance, God's atemporal existence, or owing to the fact that the occurrences of the evils in question have some indeterminacy in their causal history, such that there are no truths about these evils until they occur – still God either atemporally knows that these evils occur or God knows that these evils occur as they occur and knows ahead of time of the risk of their occurrence, given God's knowledge of the content of God's initial creative decree and God's knowledge of all the features of our world, including its natural laws, its past states, and the powers granted to created beings. Hence there are no truths about actual instances of evil and no truths about risks of evil that are unknown to God or about which God is ignorant. Since God is essentially omnipotent, God is able to do everything there is to be done, so God is able to prevent every preventable evil and, with respect to any evil there may be that is unpreventable *prior to* its occurrence owing to, for example, lack of infallible divine foreknowledge and indeterminacy in the causal history of the evil, God is able to prevent the risk of every such evil – by, for instance, not creating anything at all, or by issuing a fully determinate creative decree or by declining to give any created beings free will of a sort that requires causal indeterminism. Since God is perfectly good, God would prevent the occurrence of any evil (and any risk of evil) that God knows about and can prevent without thereby losing some greater good or permitting some evil equally bad or worse. Thus, if God exists, then there are no instances of evil which God is not justified in allowing, that is, there are no pointless evils in the world.

I take this sub-argument for the first premise of the argument from pointless evils to be successful.

1.4 Examining Premise 2 of the Argument from Pointless Evil

The second premise of the argument from pointless evils asserts that our world contains an instance (or instances of) pointless evil. For some people, this premise seems so obviously true that it stands in no need of defense. Among the times I have this impression are when I think, for instance, of the truly horrific treatment and suffering on the part of girls and women documented in Nicholas Kristof and Sheryl WuDunn's (2009) book, *Half the Sky* (among other places), including cases of brutal gang rape, virtually unspeakable deliberate physical mutilation of girls and women with sticks and acid and other weapons, dehumanizing sexual slavery, and medical complications from the reproductive process.

Consider, as one example, the suffering endured by Simeesh Segaye, who shares her account of extensive injuries sustained through pregnancy (Kristof and WuDunn, 2009, pp. 100–102). After two full days of childbirth labor, Simeesh was barely conscious and no baby had appeared. Her neighbors carried her for hours to the nearest road and put her on a bus, which took another two hours to reach a hospital, where, by then, the baby was found to be dead. Back in her village, Simeesh found that she was severely damaged, leaking urine and feces, devastated by the loss of her baby, and humiliated by the constant smell of her wastes. Her parents and husband saved for the bus fare to take her back to the hospital, but the other riders on the bus complained so vociferously about her stench that the driver ordered her off, and she had to return home. Her husband then abandoned her. Her parents kept her, but in a separate hut, in order to keep the odor away. Simeesh remained lying on the ground in the hut; food and water were brought to her, but she was alone in constant agony and wanting to die. "I just curled up," she says, "for two years." She ate little, because the more she ate or drank, the more wastes leaked down her legs. After two years of watching their daughter in her excruciating condition, starving to death, her parents sold everything they had to pay for a car to take them to a hospital a day's drive away, from which she was referred to the specialized Addis Ababa

Fistula Hospital. After the two years she had spent lying in a fetal position on the ground in the hut, Simeesh's legs had become bent, and she was too weak and emaciated to survive surgery for fistula repair. After many months of painful physical therapy, nutritious food, and a temporary colostomy, Simeesh was able to walk again and to have her fistula repaired, restoring her body, her dignity, and her will to live. I consider the days upon days that Simeesh spent curled up in a fetal position, alone on the ground in a hut, leaking urine and feces from an injury sustained during childbirth, to be a case of suffering that is not necessary for bringing about a greater good – that is, as a case of pointless evil.

Now, of course, a critic will reply that neither I nor others can legitimately allege that we "simply see" that Simeesh's suffering in her days curled up alone on the ground, leaking wastes, is pointless. (We can allege it, but we are lying or mistaken or self-deceived.) The critic might continue: perhaps one can simply see that there is the screen of a device or a book in front of one, as one reads these words, and perhaps it is a matter of common sense that one justifiably believes that there is a screen or a book in front of one, on the basis of this perception. But an absence of God-justifying reasons for an instance of evil is a very complicated sort of thing for one to allege to perceive. One can see a sweater *as red* and one can see a mug *as solid*. However, the critic objects, I cannot – and no one can – really see a case of suffering *as having no God-justifying reason.*

We can appreciate the point that a claim to seeing some event (or series of events) *as an event or events for which there could not be any God-justifying reason* is a rather complex perceptual claim. And the critic might add that it is claim that is not as widely reported among human beings as claims to see something *as red* or *as solid* or *as cylindrical.* This might indicate that we human beings have perceptual faculties for discerning features such as colors and shapes, the sorts of faculties that one can study in psychology and neuro-science. And, the critic might continue, we have no good reason for thinking that we likewise have a perceptual faculty – or, even more broadly, a cognitive faculty – that accurately tracks or picks up on the presence or absence of God-justifying reasons for the occurrence of events.

A defender of Premise 2 might say here that we do have moral faculties for perceiving events *as horrifically malicious* or *as tremendously kind* or *as unspeakably evil.* And these faculties, she might continue, enable us to see or have the impression that nothing could justify anyone who had the power, goodness, and knowledge to end (or to completely prevent or shorten the duration of) Simeesh's suffering in failing or declining to do so. I am allied with Nick Trakakis in his observation that "one of the fundamental givens of our moral experience" is that "there are evils that strike us as unredeemable, incomprehensible, and inexplicable – not in the ... sense that there are some evils that may have a point that we cannot uncover, but rather that many evils are such that they have absolutely no point at all" (Trakakis, 2013, p. 365). For many people, our experience of the world includes the impression, when confronted with certain horrific evils – such as cases of suffering in Nazi death camps, and instances in which an individual's medical surgeries result in permanent neuropathic pain that robs him of an ability to have a normal life – that "clearly no perfect being is in charge of the universe" and "God would never allow that."

Some theists may deny that they have any such impressions or experiences of the world. However, not all theists do. Meghan Sullivan, for instance, while a theist, refers to herself as among "those of us inclined to think that we are somewhat reliable detectors of the pointless evils around us" (Sullivan, 2013, p. 409). Peter van Inwagen (2006), Michael Peterson (2022), and William Hasker (1992) are additional prominent theists who accept that our world does contain instances of pointless evil. I present and discuss a different argument from evil in Section 2.2, directed toward those theists who accept – in my view, wisely – Premise 2 of the argument from pointless evil (while they deny – in my view, wrongly – Premise 1).

I have presented one type of support for premise 2 of the argument from pointless evil: namely, pointing to instances that exemplify the premise. Here is a different sub-argument for the truth of premise 2 of the argument from pointless evil. We, collectively as human beings – including theologians working in a variety of monotheistic religious traditions, historical and contemporary professional philosophers, authors of literature, religious leaders, and many of us in our ordinary lives – have aimed across the centuries to construct theodicies, that is, attempts at articulating the reason or reasons for which God would cause or allow evils in our world. As we examine those proposed theodicies, which will be given close attention in the sections to come, it becomes evident that they do not succeed in covering all instances of evil. There are some evils that, despite our working very hard, with as much diligence, care, fair-mindedness, and insight as we can to concoct reasons that might justify God in permitting them, are instances of suffering for which theodicies fail. Thus, the reasonable conclusion to reach, in light of this failed collective project, is that there are instances of pointless evil in the world.

Now, I have yet to make good on the claim that the project of theodicy fails. The project of articulating and critically examining a wide array of available theodicies will occupy Sections 3 and 4. The work in Sections 3 and 4 thus serves as a continued development of support for the argument in the previous paragraph. But first, I should pause to address in the next section a prominent theistic line of response to the argument from pointless evil I have not yet either named or rigorously examined: that is the position of skeptical theism.

2 Skeptical Theism and Arguments from Evil

In this section, skeptical theism is explored as a line of response to the argument from pointless evils, particularly its second premise. The section then explains reasons for which some theists deny the argument's first premise, namely, that if God were to exist, then there would be no pointless evils in the world. Such theists face an argument for the nonexistence of God from the facts about evil – including the amount, intensity, and distribution of evil we find in our world. I suggest reasons for thinking that skeptical theism is an unsatisfactory response to both of these arguments from evil – the argument from pointless evils and the argument from the facts about evil – thus motivating the project of theodicy.

2.1 Skeptical Theism's Reply to the Argument from Pointless Evil

There are varying articulations of skeptical theism in the literature in philosophy of religion, united not (as the name of the position might seem to suggest) by doubt about the existence of God, but rather by a shared skepticism about our human intellectual abilities when it comes to understanding the reasons for which God might cause or allow particular instances of evil to occur or the reasons for which God might cause or allow the facts about evil in our world, including its ubiquity, amount, intensity, and distribution, to be what they are. For instance, in characterizing skeptical theism, Daniel Howard-Snyder and Justin McBrayer write, "Skeptical theists are theists who are skeptical of our abilities to determine whether the evils in our world are actually pointless. If they are right, then no one is in a position to determine whether certain arguments from evil are sound" (McBrayer and Howard-Snyder, 2013, p. xiii) As Derk Pereboom describes the position, "due to the limitations of our cognitive capacities, we should be skeptical of the view that the facts about evil in the world count as good evidence against the existence of God" (Pereboom, 2013, p. 416)

Similarly, but alternatively, Paul Draper (1996) characterizes skeptical theism in part by way of the following theses: first, human beings are in no position to judge directly that an omniscient and omnipotent being would be unlikely to have a morally sufficient reason to permit the evils of the world; and second, human beings are in no position to compare the ability of the hypothesis of theism to explain certain facts about good and evil to the ability of a competing hypothesis to explain those facts. Thomas Senor somewhat differently characterizes skeptical theism as a view that emphasizes the "grand divide between divine and human understanding," acknowledging that our initial inclination is to think that a world created by God would be one that lacked horrible evils the point of which we cannot discern and that our disappointed expectation of observing such a world on an assumption of theism is "deeply troubling"; he nonetheless maintains that "a deep and well-articulated understanding of what theism says about God and humanity should remove whatever expectations we might have antecedently had about whether a world created and tended to by God would include horrors and clueless evils" (Senor, 2013, p. 428).

Michael Bergmann, a skeptical theist, too, describes skeptical theism as involving endorsement of the following theses: one, we have no good reason for thinking that the possible goods we know of are representative of the possible goods there are (ST1); two, we have no good reason for thinking that the possible evils we know of are representative of the possible evils there are (ST2); and three, we have no good reason for thinking that the entailment relations we know of between possible goods and the permission of possible evils are representative of the entailment relations there are between possible goods and the permission of possible evils (ST3) (Bergmann, 2009, p. 376.) Bergmann clarifies that, in ST1–ST3, our interest is in whether or not our sample is representative of all the possible goods, possible evils, and entailment relations there are relative to the property of figuring in a (potentially) God-justifying reason for permitting the evils we observe.

Now Michael Rea contends that a skeptical theist might endorse some of the theses in the various above characterizations of skeptical theism, but not others. He articulates the core skeptical tenet of skeptical theism – the "thesis to which all skeptical theists will agree and with which all opponents of skeptical theism will disagree" (Rea, 2013, p. 485) – as follows:

> (ST) No human being is ever justified (or warranted, or reasonable) in=thinking the following about any evil *e* that has ever occurred: there is (or is probably) no reason that could justify God in permitting *e*.
> (Rea, 2013, p. 483)

Trent Dougherty and Justin McBrayer likewise write that skeptical theists "are united in thinking that our epistemic limitations are such that no human is justified in believing that any particular evil is gratuitous" (Dougherty and McBrayer, 2014, p. vii)

Given these various characterizations in the literature, we might call skeptical theism a family of related views which have in common a commitment to the existence of God along with skepticism about our abilities as human beings to comprehend God's reasons for causing or allowing particular instances of, or the general facts about, pain and suffering in our world.

The key point I want to make here is that, arguably, (ST) is false. Rea (2013) identifies (ST) as the core thesis of skeptical theism and the claim to which all skeptical theists will agree, as do Dougherty and McBrayer in writing that skeptical theists "are united in thinking that . . . *no human is justified* in believing that any particular evil is gratuitous" (italics added). Rea, and Dougherty and McBrayer, may be mistaken about this agreement – perhaps some skeptical theists will say that they do not affirm (ST) – but if they are right about (ST) being the core thesis of skeptical theism, and if (ST) is false, then skeptical theism is undermined as a response to the argument from pointless evil.

I gave some reasons in Section 1 for thinking that some people are justified in believing of some cases of evil that they are pointless. Let me say more here. Consider the husband whose wife labors agonizingly in childbirth, only for their child to be stillborn and his wife subsequently to die of excessive bleeding after delivery. There is, from his perspective, no rhyme or reason in the death of his baby and his wife, when the infants and wives of his neighbors survive childbirth. His child was wanted; his wife was deeply loved; and now his grief and aloneness are overwhelming. He has no religious experiences of God's presence or comfort. He has not learned of any positive reasons or arguments for God's existence. His overall collection of beliefs supports the belief that, if there were a perfectly good, all-knowing, and all-powerful God who created the universe and is in charge of its operation, that God would not have allowed his wife and child to die and would not have set things up so that a natural biological process such as childbirth is both so agonizing and risks death.

Consider, too, the case of a mother whose teenage son, Matthew, is flourishing until a spinal injury makes him unable to attend school. The surgical procedure which promises to "put him back the way God made him," in the surgeon's words, creates more pain and the necessity for a cane in order to walk at all. The back brace, medically recommended, creates a deep abscess wound, the surgery for which causes a hospital-acquired staph infection, which disintegrates a large area of tissue and muscle, requiring additional surgery, which itself causes pudendal neuralgia – burning pain throughout the pelvis – making her son unable to sit. Further surgery to remove the original spinal screws, which have come loose, and to fuse sections of the spine, fails. Implantation of a spinal cord stimulator, hoped to relieve pain, also fails. Matthew is reduced to being bedbound, his future ability to earn a living and to have a family of his own uncertain, his ability to travel, to learn to drive a car, and socialize are now gone. He was, and remains, kind, empathetic, and emotionally strong, even while alone and homebound, lacking friends and in physical pain. His mother is aware of major arguments for God's existence, but she views the cosmological argument as not securing the traditional attributes of God including perfect goodness and omniscience, and she views the teleological argument as not supporting the view that there is one God, perfect in nature, given the dysfunctional aspects of the world. She has had religious experiences in the past, a sense of God's presence in worship and prayer, but over time she has come to view these as nonveridical, produced not by a real God but instead by the beauty of music at the time, a sense of the comfort of belonging to a community, and the desire for a perfect Father and for there to be an order and sense in the universe. Now, caring for her son every day, unable even to look at photos and videos of him running, dancing, and playing freely as he could in the past, she is justified in believing that her son's constant pain and disability are an instance of pointless evil. There was no rhyme or reason at all in the series of events that led to his intractable pain, no one in particular at fault, and no sense to be made of his potential to physically, professionally, and socially thrive being cut off in his early teens.

In asserting that no human being is justified in believing of any instance of evil that it is pointless, the skeptical theist who endorses (ST) is claiming that no descendent of a victim of the Holocaust is justified in believing that his ancestors' suffering and premature deaths were unnecessary for bringing about a greater good; that no survivor of sexual assault is justified in believing that there is no reason that could justify God in remaining inert during her brutal assault; and that no parent of a child murdered in the mass school shooting in Uvalde, Texas, is justified in believing that their child's death was pointless. This seems to me to be an extraordinarily absurd claim. Such individuals who suffer themselves and whose loved ones suffer can be justified in their beliefs in pointlessness, given the overall structure of their other beliefs, which may include reasoning of the sorts set out above concerning the tensions between God and evil and the failure of justificatory attempts. If the claim at the core of skeptical theism were that some people are justified in believing that all instances of evil are permitted by God for justifying reasons, that would be a different matter and still would remain to be shown. What is simply wholly implausible is the claim that no human being is ever justified in believing of any instance of evil that it is pointless.

Let me try to say something on behalf of the skeptical theist here. Perhaps in the cases I have given, individuals do think that their own, or their loved one's, suffering or early death is pointless, but they are not *justified* in thinking so, since they are failing to appreciate the vast gulf in perspective and information between an omniscient being, on the one hand, and beings limited in perspective and information, like ourselves, on the other. Our understanding in relation to God's has been compared, by Stephen Wykstra (1984) and other skeptical theists, to that of tiny infants in relation to adult human beings, in virtue of our limited ability to comprehend the ways of God and the reasons of God for acting, or declining to act, as God does. Just as infants have no choice but to trust their caregivers to meet their needs and we should not expect infants to understand their caregivers' reasoning and behavior, so too should we simply trust God and not expect that we, with the limitations of our location in a particular space and time, and the limitations of our knowledge, concepts, and reasoning capacities, could understand the reasoning and ways of God. Our knowledge is limited; God's is unlimited. An adequate appreciation of this difference should lead every human being to acknowledge, says the skeptical theist who endorses (ST), that every time we are tempted to think that some instance of evil is pointless, we should check ourselves and realize that such a belief is unjustified. We could not possibly know, or even justifiably believe, regarding any case of evil, that there is no reason or set of reasons that could justify God in causing or allowing it. God is too far beyond us in order for any such belief of ours to be justified.

Here, in defense of the skeptical theist's viewpoint, we might bring in a principle articulated by Wykstra (1984, p. 85), dubbed the Condition on ReasoNable Epistemic Access (CORNEA), which states that, on the basis of a cognized situation S, a particular human person is entitled to claim "it appears that p" only if it is reasonable for her to believe that, given her cognitive faculties and the use she has made of them, if p were not the case, then the cognized situation S would likely be different than it is in some way discernible to her. So as to avoid ambiguities in the term 'appears' in this original formulation and to focus on justified beliefs rather than entitlements to claim, we could put the idea (or a closely related idea) in this way: we are only justified in believing that a situation really is as we perceive it to be if it is reasonable for us to believe that, if the situation were not really as we (currently) perceive it to be, we could tell this – our perception or experience of the situation would be different. To see the application to the present debate over pointless evils, we could express the (or a closely related) idea in this way: we are only justified in believing that something is not there from our perception that it is not there if we have good reason for thinking that, if it were there, we would see it. A skeptical theist may allege that we do not have good reason for thinking that, if God-justifying reasons for permitting instances of evil were there, we would see them (see Wykstra, 1996). We do have good reason for thinking that, if a horse were in our bedroom, we would see it. But we do not have good reason for thinking that, if COVID-19 viral particles were hanging in the air in the produce area of our grocery store, we would see them. The skeptical theist may maintain that God's reasons are more like the

COVID-19 particles, in being (cognitively or perceptually) invisible to us, than they are like visible horses.

In response, first, I think that CORNEA and principles closely related to it threaten to undermine the defensibility of belief in God based in religious experience. Notice that, according to CORNEA, a human person is entitled to claim that it appears that God is present in a certain worship service she is taking part in only if it is reasonable for her to believe that, if God were not present in the worship service, her cognized situation would be different in a discernible way. But arguably it is not reasonable to believe that, given what we know about the powers of group thinking in crowds, the sway of rhetoric and moving music and religious imagery in stained glass and art, the force of emotions such as fear and regret and hope, the power of desires for connection and love, the force of wishful thinking, and the role of psychological and social needs in the interpretation of our experiences.

More pertinent to the present discussion, I do not think the line of response articulated just above works to support skeptical theism. Perhaps it is true that we are only justified in believing that something is not there from our perception that it is not there if we have good reason for thinking that, if it were there, we would see it. But I think we *do* have good reasons for thinking that, if there were God-justifying reasons for the instances of evil in question, we would see them. One is that we are rational and moral beings, like God. (I defend elsewhere [Ekstrom, 2021, chapter 6] the view that God is a perfectly morally good being against a conception of God, such as Mark Murphy's (2017) conception, as perfectly good but not perfectly morally good.) We are the sorts of beings who can discern moral reasons and who are attentive to the matter of what is morally justified and what is morally unjustified. We adult human beings are not infantile as moral agents. We have quite a good grasp on what is good – for example, pleasure, love, knowledge, personal life, safety, health, peace, joy – and on what is bad – for example, pain, racial hatred, child abuse, and the premature death of persons. We think enormously hard about ethical principles and about how to handle moral dilemmas, and with respect to what goods there are, what evils there are, and when it is and is not justifiable to permit some evil in order to bring about a greater good, we are not clueless. On theism, we are made in the image of God, as rational beings who can have knowledge, including of moral truths and about God, supporting belief in our rational and moral powers. (See also Peterson, 2022, pp. 23–25.)

A second reason is that, on theism, God wants for us to love and trust God, to be in close personal relationship with God. Love and trust in personal relationships involve the protection of the well-being of the other and the sharing of reasons for what we do, especially when it involves causing pain or loss to the one we love. When we must allow someone we love to suffer for the sake of bringing about a greater good, such as when we take our children to get vaccinations and medical procedures, we explain to them what is happening and why we are allowing their suffering, and we assure them throughout of our love, our reasons, our presence, and the greater end. It is therefore reasonable to think that, if God were there, loving us and wanting us to know and trust God, God would communicate to us the reasons for which God causes or allows us to endure what we do.

2.2 An Argument from the Facts about Evil

Let me turn to addressing a theist who *grants* that there are pointless evils in our world but who does not take their existence to undercut the rationality of belief in God. As I mentioned in Section 1, Peter van Inwagen is one such prominent theist, as are William Hasker and Michael Peterson, among others. Van Inwagen aims to show that, even if God does exist, there can be some instances of evil in the world that are pointless, in the sense that there is no particular God-justifying reason for which God permits *that* precise instance of evil itself to occur, as opposed to some different particular evil of the same type, instead. So, for example, even if God exists, there may exist no God-justifying reason for which Simeesh's suffering from physical injuries sustained in the process of childbirth is permitted to occur, instead of a different woman (say, Simeesh's neighbor) suffering similar injuries in the process of childbirth. Likewise, there may be no God-justifying reason for the permission of a particular person's being the victim of sexual assault rather than a different person, instead.

Van Inwagen suggests that there may be (and for all we know there is) indeterminacy or chanciness concerning which particular evils occur in our world, owing to several factors, including indeterminacy in God's initial decree concerning which among a variety of possible worlds is made actual (such that, God's initial creative decree is not of the form "Let world A be," but rather "Let world A or B or C or D or E ... be"), as well as natural indeterminacy, and indeterminacy stemming from the power of free will granted to created beings. Hence, on van Inwagen's view, it is consistent with the nature of God that our world has instances of pointless evil in it. God may exist and yet be unjustified in allowing a particular instance of actual evil, because neither that token of evil itself, nor the risk of its occurring, in particular (such as Matthew's surgery going awry, resulting in lasting neuropathic pain), was necessary for a greater good. It could be the case (and for all we know it is the case) that what was necessary for the greater good is that some evil or other like the instance of pointless evil occur, an evil of its type, or the risk of there being evils of its type (such as our having nervous systems susceptible to chronic pain or there being medical surgeries that cause permanent nerve damage). And this more global justification, van Inwagen contends, is sufficient for upholding the perfection of God.

From my perspective, the global justifications van Inwagen offers for the evils in the world are not sufficient for maintaining God's perfection. This is because, on van Inwagen's account, God leaves sentient and rational beings at the mercy of chance, such that we are subject both to good luck and to horrifically bad luck. It seems to me that a perfectly good being who is worthy of love, trust, and worship would not do this to us. If God were to exist as the perfect being God is supposed to be, arguably God would not leave us in a chancy world, subjected to the bad luck of randomness in the initial divine decree, bad luck due to indeterminacy in the natural world, and bad luck deriving from the indeterminist free will granted to created beings. In my view it is cruel to create sentient and rational beings and to leave them at the mercy of chance. On van Inwagen's picture, one is supposed to love, trust, and revere a God who might let one be raped, murdered, incapacitated by a degenerative disease, or made to endure daily intractable pain, even though there is no particular reason whatsoever for one to suffer in such a way. There is only the general reason that such a world (allegedly, for all we know) is better overall than a world in which people do not experience such calamities as a matter of indeterminism. This does not seem to me a tenable position. We do not let our own beloved children loose in a forest filled with rapists, buried land mines, and trees that might crash on them, so far as we are able.

Nonetheless, suppose I were wrong about this, and suppose it were perfectly consistent with God's existence for there to be pointless evils and rational to believe in God even in the face of pointless evils. There are theists who accept the existence of pointless evils in our world. As a challenge to such theists, we may offer the following, different, argument from evil for the nonexistence of God.

Argument from the Facts about Evil:

(1) If God were to exist, then certain global facts about evil in our world would not obtain, including the vast amount of suffering, the intensity of suffering in truly horrid cases, and the distribution of suffering among sentient and rational beings.

(2) These facts about evil in our world do obtain, including the vast amount of suffering, the intensity of suffering in truly horrid cases, and the distribution of suffering there is.

(3) Therefore, God does not exist.

2.3 Support for Premise 1 of the Argument from the Facts about Evil

The facts about evil in our world – its amount, intensity, and distribution – simply are what they are. Evaluation of the argument from the facts about evil, then, turns on assessment of its first premise. Why would one think that Premise 1 of the argument is true? Here is a case in its favor, which cannot be made good in a single paragraph, but which will be developed over the course of this and the subsequent two sections. After prolonged and rigorous reflection on various proposals concerning the reasons that allegedly justify God in permitting evil in the amount and of the kinds and in the distribution we observe in the world, we find none that are particularly compelling or satisfactory. There are not other persuasive suggestions in the vast literature on the problem of evil concerning what the God-justifying reasons for these facts might be. Thus the facts about evil concerning its amount, distribution, and kinds are facts for which there are not God-justifying reasons. But if God were to exist, then there would be God-justifying reasons for the obtaining of these facts, or else these facts would not obtain. But these facts do obtain. Therefore, God does not exist. As Rowe expresses the thought with regard to the variety and amount of suffering we find, "In light of our experience and knowledge of the variety and scale of human and animal suffering in our world, the idea that none of this suffering could have been prevented by an omnipotent being without thereby losing a greater good or permitting an evil at least as bad seems an extraordinarily absurd idea, quite beyond our belief" (Rowe, 1979, p. 338).

I concur with Rowe. The thrust of the argument is that, if a perfectly good, perfectly knowledgeable, and all-powerful Creator and sustainer of the world were to exist, then there would not be as much suffering, cruelty, disease, and atrocity as there is, on the immense scale that characterizes genocides and global pandemics, and there would not be such intense instances of suffering and cruelty as there are – in sustained torturous child abuse and the heinous treatment of enslaved persons, for example. Moreover, there would not be the distribution of suffering among human beings and other sentient beings that is characterized by some lives (even of those who are vicious) being charmed with health and prosperity, while into other lives (even of those who are kind, empathic, and giving) are piled calamity upon injury upon victimization upon loss. The supposition that, if there were a God who created our universe, *there could not be less evil*, and *there could not be less intense evils*, and *there could not be a less unfair distribution of evils*, without thereby losing a greater good, seems simply not credible.

2.4 Skeptical Theism's Reply to the Argument from the Facts about Evil

In response to the argument from the facts about evil, a skeptical theist may deny that we can justifiably believe that there are not God-justifying reasons for the obtaining of the facts about evil and so deny the premise that, if God were to exist, then the facts about evil would not obtain. Recall Pereboom's description of skeptical theism as the view that, "due to the limitations of our cognitive capacities, we should be skeptical of the view that the facts about evil in the world count as good evidence against the existence of God"(Pereboom, 2013, p. 416). Similarly, Draper characterizes skeptical theism in part by the thesis that human beings are in no position to compare the power of the hypothesis of theism "to explain certain facts about good and evil" to the ability of a competing hypothesis, such as naturalism, to explain those facts (Draper, 1996) Our (allegedly) being in no good position to make such a comparison or to reach the conclusion that God does not exist in light of the facts about evil is said to derive from the limitations of our cognitive capacities.

Let's think for a minute about this cluster of ideas concerning our cognitive capacities in relation to God. Consider someone who adopts the *skeptical* aspect of skeptical theism and who also adopts the *theism* aspect of skeptical theism. What I want to bring to the fore is the impression that this mindset exhibits a somewhat bizarre mismatch between intellectual humility and intellectual self-assurance. The skeptical theist makes a bold speculative metaphysical claim, that God exists, one that has broad implications for a person's way of life – including habits of worship, (oftentimes) political views, attitudes toward other people, daily actions including prayers of gratitude and prayers of supplication, social networks, sense of mission, and (sometimes) claims to land, among others – and yet he professes intellectual timidity, ineptitude or inadequacy, with respect to explaining or understanding experienced and observed suffering. The skeptical theist takes his cognitive capacities to be up to the task of knowing – or at least to committing to the proposition in a way that has profound implications for his way of life – that an absolutely perfect supernatural being exists, one who created and sustains the universe. Yet in the face of the facts about evil in the world, he takes his cognitive capacities to be too limited to reason well. Is this not an odd sort of amalgam of attitudes toward the human intellect?

To put the point another way: in response to such a profound metaphysical question as, "Does God exist?," the theist stakes his claim with those who say "Yes!" (one might envision this with the stamp of a fist, although it need not be; it is, at least, placement of oneself as standing in the camp of theists.) But in the face of the facts about evil in our world, the skeptical theist gives a humble shrug. (The "shrug" is not meant to suggest that the skeptical theist does not *care* about evils but rather that his attitude is one that says, "Who am I to say? My mind is not up to the task of understanding.") This is a rather striking incongruity, I find, between belief in the positive power of one's cognitive capacities, on the one hand, and belief in their lack of power, on the other.

A skeptical theist might say at this juncture: look, here I am already believing in God, for reasons of my own, centrally that I've judged theism to make best sense of my experience of the world, and now you come and bother me by putting in my face the facts about evil in our world, alleging that these throw into question the rationality of my belief in God. He might continue: part of my set of religious beliefs is that God is infinitely wiser than I am, and is infinitely good, and so has reasons for permitting the things that happen in the world, including allowing so much suffering and of the kinds and in the distribution it is, and these are reasons that I should not expect to understand, given my limited (and sinful) nature as a human being.

Of course, we can understand the feeling of bother or affront this skeptical theist expresses, and if we have been or are currently theists, we can relate to it. But surely it is fair for one to ask: How can a skeptical theist (sensibly) accept theism as making best sense of his experience of the world, when – unless he lives in a kind of utopia-type sub-situation of the world wholly isolated from historical information, access to news and the arts and other expressions of human experience – his experience of the world includes not only suffering on a personal level but also general acquaintance with the facts about evil in our world? It does not seem right to say that a sufficient theistic answer to reasoning expressed in the argument from the facts about evil is this: I am clueless about why those facts are as they are – why there are evils on the scale of the Holocaust and the Rwandan genocide, for example, and why some people suffer so intensely and have their lives marred by injuries after injustices after illnesses that continue to pile on – but my belief in God *got here first*, and that belief indicates that I should not expect to have a clue.[2] Notice that it is not, of course, as if the facts about evil in the world intend themselves to annoy theists, and it is not as if anyone who articulates the reasoning encapsulated in the argument from the facts about evil does so solely in order to annoy those who believe in God. We all, in common as human beings, experience and observe the facts

---

[2] Derk Pereboom helpfully suggests that a way forward for a theist here is not to profess cluelessness but perhaps to combine a somewhat lowered rational credence in theism with hope or faith, along with offering "some indication of what the goods might be that justify God in permitting evil – perhaps partial reasons ... gleaned from various theodicies," such as those explored in Sections 3 and 4 of this Element. See Pereboom, 2013, pp. 416–422, at p. 421.

about evil in our world, and we should all be deeply perplexed about, and form our beliefs in part in light of, these facts. In response to the skeptical theist's thought, articulated in the previous paragraph, I am reminded of Hasker's remark that, if one views the problem of evil "primarily as a group of arguments devised by atheists to make life difficult for theists," then perhaps a deflective or purely defensive response might be sufficient. "But if one is deeply troubled and perplexed by the actual phenomena of evil," he continues, then what "one needs, in that case, is some positive account of evil, something that offers some actual understanding of why evil exists and how it fits into God's plan for the world. In other words, a theodicy" (Hasker, 1998, p. 62.) I entirely agree with Hasker on this point.

The skeptical theist might not be satisfied that we have fully appreciated the logic of his position. Here is one way he might proceed. I adopt, he might say, a Plantinga-inspired externalist epistemological account on which one can know that God exists if one believes that God exists and if this belief is warranted and if this belief is true (Plantinga, 2000). One's belief in God is warranted just in case it is produced by a faculty that is functioning properly, as designed, in an appropriate environment. I believe, he continues, that we human beings have this faculty, a *sensus divinitatis*, given to us by God in order that we may know God. I couple this account of knowledge of God with what I view as an appropriate appreciation of human cognitive limitations, such as those named by William Alston (1991) and by Michael Bergmann (2009). I can reasonably think that God exists and that I can know this by way of properly functioning mental faculties, while at the same time acknowledging that human beings are not omniscient and are limited in particular ways that are applicable to the evaluation of arguments from evil. For example, Bergmann's theses (ST1–ST3) (Section 2.1) are plausible ones, from my perspective, and so I am not justified (and neither are you) in thinking of any particular instance of evil that it is pointless, and I am not justified (and neither are you) in thinking that, if God were to exist, then there would not be evils in the amounts, intensity, and distribution that there are.

In response, first, arguably Bergmann's theses (ST1–ST3) are highly implausible, in part for reasons given above concerning our individual and collective intelligent moral agency and, on theism, our having been created in God's image to enter into relationships of love, trust, and mutual understanding with God. (For further argumentation, see Hasker 2010; Ekstrom 2021; Peterson 2022.) Second, notice that a theist who believes that we have faculties for discerning God's presence and God's agency, divinely given human faculties which deliver such beliefs as, *God is filling me with joy at this moment* and *God is granting me a feeling of forgiveness in assurance of my salvation* and

God is moving me to share the Gospel with this person – in other words, divine presence appearances or religious experiences that ground a theistic structure of beliefs – already believes that he has insight into God's actions, God's ways, and God's intentions and purposes. Such a theist's believing that we have truth-directed perceptual, cognitive, and moral faculties seems to me to provide him with reason to think that we can discern God's reasons for what God does (for instance, *God is comforting me to show me his love*) and God's reasons for what God allows (*God permits me to have doubts and endure trials in order to strengthen my patience and test my endurance in my faith*). In response to the question of why beliefs such as *God made this beautiful canyon* would count as rationally justified but not the belief *Simeesh's days of suffering alone in the hut are unnecessary for a greater good* or the belief *the world contains too much suffering for there to be a perfect being in charge of it*, Plantinga and Plantinga-inspired theists answer: because the latter beliefs are not produced by the *sensus divinitatis*, but are caused instead by sin and dysfunction in intellectual faculties.

I wonder, what is one supposed to say in response to the theist who asserts this: if you think there are any pointless evils in the world, or if you think that there are not God-justifying reasons for the facts about evil in the world, or if you think that if God were to exist then the facts of evil would not be as they are, your cognitive faculties are malfunctioning, due to your sin? One reply is that they do not seem to be malfunctioning. My moral, intellectual, and perceptual faculties are intact. A second reply is this: the claim that my thinking as I do is due to cognitive derangement stemming from my sin stops the conversation. It seems fair to ask in response, could you show me, instead, the error in my reasoning? In my view, we all, theists and nontheists alike, should aim to have defensible knowledge, involving beliefs that we rationally justify to others by way of offering reasons for them and by way of defending them against theoretical objections. Beliefs that get their warrant as Plantinga describes still have to be able to meet defeaters. As a rational agent, one ought to do more than simply saying, *if* theism (in particular, Christianity) is true and *if* Plantinga's account of knowledge is correct, then my belief in God is warranted – and it seems to me that theism (in particular, Christianity) is true.

2.5 Motivation for the Project of Theodicy

The argument from pointless evil and the argument from the facts about evil stand as powerful arguments against the existence of God. I have suggested that skeptical theism is a problematic and unsatisfactory response to these arguments. If it is theoretically rational to believe that God exists, then some positive arguments in favor of God's existence must be stronger than the arguments from evil against God's existence, and some theodicy or collection of theodicies must explain why God, an omniscient, omnipotent, perfectly good being, allows or causes the instances of suffering in our world to occur and the facts about evil to be what they are. The project of close consideration of positive arguments for God's existence – including the cosmological, teleological, and ontological arguments and arguments based in religious experience – deserves and has other venues. Here, in the subsequent two sections, I concentrate on the part of defending the rationality of theism that involves articulating theodicies, attempted explanations of the reasons that justify God in permitting the evils of our world.

3 Theodicies: Contrast, Character, Punishment, and Free Will

In this section, we begin to explore a wide range of theodicies. The term 'theodicy' stems from the Greek words *theos*, meaning God, and *dike*, meaning justice. A theodicy is an attempt to show how the justice and goodness of God can be upheld in the face of the evils in our world by articulating the reasons that justify God in permitting instances of evil to occur and the reasons that justify God in causing or allowing the facts about evil in our world to be what they are. Providing explanation of the reasons for which God is justified in permitting the instances of evil in the world enables the theodicist to counter the claim that there are pointless evils in the world; and articulating God's reasons for causing or allowing the facts of evil in our world to be what they are empowers the theodicist to counter the first premise of the argument from the facts about evil for the nonexistence of God.

3.1 Contrast and Appreciation

When conversations in philosophy classrooms and among our friends and families turn to questions about suffering and God, one thought that inevitably get articulated centers on the idea of contrast between good and evil. The suggestion made is that, without evil, including pain, suffering, and wrong-doing, there could not be good. Good and evil are two sides of a coin, so to speak. The idea is that good and evil must *both* exist – one of them could not exist if the other did not exist to be a contrast to it. The interlocutor urges, what is light without darkness, or up without down?

But we should tease apart two different lines of thinking here. One asserts that good and evil must both exist if either does; one cannot be real if the other is not real. A problem for this idea is that many individuals believe in heaven, a place or a type of existence in which there is only goodness and joy and peace, no suffering or pain or anguish or discord. And it seems clear that heaven can exist even if there is no hell – not all theists who believe in heaven believe in hell, after all – and it seems clear that heaven – a purely good place or type of existence encompassing joy, love, and awe in the presence of the pure goodness of God – can exist independently, even if there is no suffering of any kind in existence at all (or any longer). Another example is the Garden of Eden: if it is coherent to envision that there is a place of pure harmony between human beings and other living things, including harmony between human beings and God, with no natural disasters or illness and no evil at all (prior to the fall of the serpent or Satan), then good can exist without evil. Here is another problem for the "necessity of contrast" line of theodicy: consider the view of billions of human beings who say that they believe in a perfect God who created the universe. Part of this view is the idea that God existed *before* the physical universe existed and that God exists *independently* of the created universe. God exists always and would exist even if God had not created the physical universe in which we live. If this belief about God is true or is even coherent, then good can exist without evil. In saying that God is or even may be the cause of the physical universe, we are acknowledging that something wholly good can exist on its own, without the need for there to be any evil in existence as a counterpart or contrast.

One might pivot at this point to expressing a line of thought that is connected but a bit different, which is that, if we human beings did not ever suffer, then we would not appreciate the good things in life, such as health, kindness, and love. On this line of reasoning, it is not that evil has to exist in order for good *to exist*, but rather that evil has to exist in order for us to *appreciate* goodness.

There is an accurate empirical observation within this line of thought, which is this: we human beings do often take for granted our health and our abilities to do the things we want to do until we get sick or injured. And then if we get well or regain our abilities, we appreciate our health and our bodies' functioning in deeper ways than we did before. We may come to have a greater sense of wellness, or an energizing sense of a new lease on life, after going through a difficult time. We might tend to savor the time we have with people we love more than we did before. So, it does seem to be true for many of us that we appreciate the good in our lives more than we would have if we had not gone through some pain, setback, or trial.

The problem is that this theodicy does not really answer the problem of why God would create beings who suffer. The reason it does not get around the theological problem is that, in thinking about God, we are considering an absolutely perfect divine being, one who could create the universe and the living beings in it in any way God pleases. God – a perfectly powerful and knowledgeable being who could create in any way – could have made living beings who do not have the psychological tendency that we human beings have, not to fully appreciate good except when and after they suffer. In other words, God could just as well make beings who are full of deep and joyful appreciation of all the goodness in the universe, all the time, without them having to suffer pain, agony, and loss. God could make created beings who richly savor their health and well-being, as well as their loving relationships and physical abilities, without their having to become sick or injured or alone or disabled at all. If there is a limitation in human psychology that makes us underappreciate goodness until we experience badness, then God, a perfect creator, could simply make different beings instead of us: beings who do not have this tendency but who instead are fully appreciative of goodness all the time. Additionally, there is the point that, if contrast were needed for appreciation of, for instance, good health and full physical functioning, then a bad dream about getting the flu or being in a car accident would be better than there being real illnesses and injuries (van Inwagen, 2006, p. 69), and atrocities on the scale of the genocides that have occurred in our world are not needed for appreciation of human dignity and cooperation.

In sum, the "contrast" and "appreciation" lines of reasoning are not convincing as attempts to make sense of the suffering that exists along with belief in God. (For insightful further critical discussion, see McBrayer, 2013).

3.2 Developing Character

There is a different a line of theodicy prominently developed by philosopher and theologian John Hick (1978), which is referred to as the "character building" or the "soul making" theodicy. The core idea is that God deliberately put us in a world that contains natural disasters and wrongdoing and pain, in order to help us grow, so that we become better people and more godlike in character over time. Hick suggests that, as our perfectly loving and good Creator, God wants us to have generosity, tenacity, persistence, patience, kindness, and other good character traits, and these develop through the process of dealing with losses and tribulations. The justifying reason for which God creates us in a world with setbacks, disappointments, and even horrific evils, in other words, is to offer us opportunities to choose to respond to them in ways that make us better people, so that we can become more courageous and more compassionate toward ourselves and others through the challenges we and others endure. If one views human beings as inherently selfish and unfit while we are on Earth to be in the presence of a holy God, one might think of the development through suffering we undergo during earthly life as a process that helps us to become less unfit to be in God's presence, a process that helps us to mature in spirit and in moral character so that we can later enter heaven and be with God.

Notice that there is an accurate empirical observation in this line of theodicy, too, which is that many people do improve their characters through enduring suffering: they become more kind or generous or perseverant, and less focused on themselves and on what material possessions they can acquire. We can and do often grow spiritually and morally when we endure hardship. We may become less self-centered. We may learn what is really important in life. We may come to have an expanded vision of the world, including forming new empathy for people in poverty and those who suffer in natural disasters and in war. People who may have been mean-spirited or selfish before becoming ill or injured or enduring some other injustice or challenge sometimes become leaders of positive movements for change, or advocates for others' rights, or fundraisers for charitable causes.

We might pose a challenge for this line of theodicy akin to the objection we posed to the appreciation theodicy: namely, that God could, instead, have created us morally mature, noble, kind, loving, and good from the start, rather than requiring us to develop these traits through time in an environment filled with dangers and pain. Consider this possibility: if God wanted to create beings with whom he could have fellowship or relationships of shared love and joy, God might have created us "fit" to be in God's presence from the start. There does not seem to be any logical requirement on God's creation of rational beings that those beings must by nature be selfish or short-sighted or unkind, beings who need to struggle through suffering and loss in order to develop good character traits.

Hick has a response to this objection, which is that, in his judgment, the good character traits that are freely developed through time in an extended process of coping with struggle and pain are *more valuable than* the good character traits which God, in our hypothetical alternative, could have given us instead, namely, good character traits possessed without requiring free responses in a temporally extended process of moral development through a world filled with suffering. Hick admits that this value judgment cannot be defended (Hick, 1978, p. 256).

A different line of objection to the character-development theodicy is to point out that, although some people do become, for instance, more courageous from facing danger, or more generous after experiencing poverty, lots of people do *not* grow through suffering. Some people who suffer simply become bitter or angry or mean. Hick has a reply to this objection, too, which is that his claim is not that every instance of suffering produces character growth, but rather that a world filled with suffering and trials is one in which created person are offered *opportunities* to freely respond by intentionally developing their characters in good ways. If we become bitter or even more selfish through suffering, that is not God's fault but ours. The emphasis in the character-building theodicy on God's offer of opportunities for, rather than guarantees of, positive moral development brings to the fore the reliance of Hick's line of theodicy on the suggestion that God gave created beings free will, enabling them to freely choose among available options regarding how to act, including the opportunity to respond poorly.

We might, still, press our objection with regard to people who do not grow through suffering. Hick suggests that evil offers opportunities for freely chosen virtuous responses. But some examples in human experience clearly do not to provide any opportunity for character development to those who suffer, including those who die prematurely, such as infants and young children who drown or suffer fatal diseases, and people who die suddenly of heart attacks and strokes, leaving them no chance to grow. Some traumas, too, are so devastating that those who undergo them are psychologically utterly destroyed, and we should not blame them by saying that their traumas gave them opportunities to grow that they themselves failed to take advantage of by effort and free choice if it was not physically or psychologically possible for them to do so in the circumstances. In addition, consider the severe and inhumane violence inflicted on human beings during the transatlantic slave trade, and on victims of the Holocaust, and on those who endure prolonged and unspeakable child abuse. It is simply not credible that a perfect God allows such horrors so that the victims have opportunities to develop their characters.

A theodicist might respond here by saying, as Richard Swinburne (1998, p. 101) does, that the victims in such horrible cases as the transatlantic slave trade are granted the good of *being of use* as the vehicle of a good purpose, such as providing other people with opportunities for freely chosen character development. I find this not plausible, as it depicts God as violating appropriate moral constraints regarding respect for the inherent dignity and value of each individual human being, particularly in cases in which being of use is nonvoluntary. If it is true that persons should each be treated as ends in themselves and never as means, then an absolutely perfect being would know this truth and would make choices concerning what to cause and allow in accordance with it. Preserving the goodness of God requires that the suffering of *victims* be good *for them*, and the alleged good of being of use is not sufficiently good for the victims of such evils as genocides, plagues, slave trades, and sexual abuse in order to provide a God-justifying reason for permitting their suffering. The requirement I have articulated in the previous sentence is known in the literature on the problem of evil as a victim-centered constraint on plausible theodicies and, while it is not agreed to by all theists, it certainly strikes many of us as a reasonable moral judgment applicable to a perfectly good and loving God who created and cares for each of us.

Even if victim-centered constraints on theodicies were rejected, the critic of the character-building theodicy may press the point that the good (such as the good of opportunities for soul-making provided to others) enabled by the suffering of victims must outweigh the negative value of the suffering which the theodicist suggests is necessary for it, and the good must pertain to human beings. With respect to outweighing, an advocate of the soul-making theodicy needs to support the contention that the temporally extended free development of good character traits is more valuable than a nontemporally extended acquisition of good character traits and is also more valuable than a temporally extended development of good character traits in a way that is not free in the sense Hick relies upon. The latter is the case because we could, alternatively, grow through time in kindness and depth of love and Godlike goodness without these developments happening as a result of human free choices of a sort that requires indeterminism and the availability of horrendously evil options. Regarding the contention in the first sentence of this paragraph that the proposed good must pertain to human beings, the point I am emphasizing is that it would not be a plausible suggestion for the theist to say that victims of the transatlantic slave trade and victims of the COVID-19 pandemic suffered for the opportunity for character development by occupants of another planet, nor would it be a plausible suggestion that they suffered for the opportunity for character development for God, since God is by nature already and consistently perfectly good.

Now the theist may suggest that, for *some* cases of suffering in our world, God is providing an opportunity for that person's character to improve, but when we observe the wide range and intensity of atrocities in the world, it certainly does not look as if all of them could be accounted for on these grounds. Would a perfect God allow your daughter or your sister to be raped and murdered so as to develop her character (or so as to develop the offender's character, or your character)? It seems mistaken and morally repellant to suggest so. The character-building theodicy, at the least, needs supplementation by other lines of theodicy in order to account for the facts about evil in our world.

3.3 Punishment for Sin

When we are enduring a loss or painful time, we sometimes ask ourselves what we did to deserve it, implicitly accepting that we brought on the condition ourselves or that it was sent to us as a kind of divine punishment. It is (sadly) rather common, too, to be treated by others as if one must have done something wrong in order to deserve one's poverty, disability, or illness. We see this illustrated in the book of Job. When Job is in the midst of enduring horrific losses, including the death of his family members, the destruction of his belongings, and the ruin of his good health, his companions urge him to repent and to beg God for forgiveness for all he has done wrong. Job is told that he is at fault and must get right with God so that he can be restored to a blessed condition. It is evidently attractive to some to believe that those who suffer have done something to deserve it and that if the victims would stop and repent, their suffering would end.

This line of thought on which some evil is penalty has been offered as a theodicy for centuries, including prominently in the work of St. Augustine and St. Thomas Aquinas. The works of these medieval theorists suggest that some of the evils in our world constitute punishments for human sin. Augustine conceived of evil not as an entity that has being in itself, although this does not mean (oddly to contemporary ears) that evil is illusory – people do suffer, and people do sin, Augustine acknowledged. Rather, on his view, evil is not a thing that has being in itself. It is not a substance that makes up part of the universe (Augustine, 1977, p. 174). Still, evil as a privation or lack of goodness exists, as degradation, damage, or defect. Augustine viewed evil as originating in the world from the wrong use of the free will, which was given by God to finite created beings. Through the fall of humankind in the original sin of Adam and Eve in the Garden of Eden, all of humanity, Augustine asserts, is guilty of sin and merits condemnation (Augustine, 1950, xiii, 14). Aquinas calls privation of form and integrity in free creatures "evil of penalty," because he, too, viewed such privations as penalties resulting both from original sin and from personal sin, and also because these privations have a characteristic feature of punishment, in that they are contrary to the will of the person who is afflicted, that is, the privation is not something the sufferer wants or chooses. Privation of due operation performed voluntarily Aquinas calls "evil of fault" because he sees the agent as at fault for the defect in the agent's free act. Of these two sorts of evil, Aquinas thinks evil of fault is worse (Aquinas, 1920, 1.49.6).

The contemporary philosopher Richard Swinburne (1998) articulates the idea that punishment is one good that could justify God in permitting the suffering of human beings. He writes: "It is good that God should provide humans with deterrents to sin . . . . Humans are weak. They need to be encouraged to do objectively good acts; and to start with, that may involve providing reasons for doing such acts additional to the reason of their intrinsic goodness, tying the performance of such acts to lower-grade self-centered rewards and punishments" (Swinburne, 1998, p. 198). After all, Swinburne continues, "parents and other educators encourage good behavior by threats and rewards as a preliminary to children learning to do good for its own sake. And it would be good for God to do the same" (Swinburne, 1998, p. 198). In this passage, punishment is depicted more as something good used for the purposes of instruction and moral conditioning, meant to guide us toward choosing to act in morally upright ways, than it is depicted as retribution that is deserved. Swinburne's approach to theodicy is also multifaceted, broader than a mere appeal to divine punishment.

There can be attraction in the punishment line of theodicy when we think about fairness, particularly with respect to fellow citizens who cheat on their taxes, or with respect to abusive spouses, or with respect to dictators and serial killers who perform heinous acts. For some people, there is a plausibility in the claim that God would rightfully hold wrongdoers accountable, punishing them with suffering, either in this life or in an afterlife, for the suffering they have inflicted on their victims.

However, the punishment theodicy is at best incomplete and cannot be a full story on its own. For one reason, the theodicist needs to explain God's justification for allowing not only suffering but also wrongdoing. For another, we observe many cases of suffering on the part of individuals who cannot, for all we can tell, deserve what happens to them, such as in cases of inherited genetic diseases, physically and emotionally abusive injuries suffered by children, childhood cancers, and nonhuman animal suffering in the wild and as a result of human cruelty. It is not credible that the sufferers in these cases suffer as just deserts for their sins in order for God to tip back the scales of justice. A punishment theodicist might appeal to original sin with regard to the suffering of infants and very young children, although this sits in tension with many of our intuitions about what very young human beings deserve (namely, loving care).

Notice that, unless one did something such as deliberately setting one's own arm on fire or jumping off a bridge (and inadvertently living anyway), it seems clear that one is not causally or morally responsible for a medical condition such as persistent pain, disease, or injury. And even if one did something like one of those actions deliberately – trying to harm oneself or to take one's own life – still one is probably not morally responsible for that, either, because mental health crises and mind-altering intolerable pain can undermine one's capacities as a responsible agent at the time. One might point out that, in some cases, there are steps in the causal processes that lead to a person's illness, injury, or pain that may count as actions for which that person is responsible – electing to go skydiving, or freely choosing to have a cosmetic surgical procedure, or selecting to go to a particular doctor – but none of those alone makes for moral responsibility for the outcome when it is horrible. It is an implausible suggestion that a person would be punished by God with multiple painful broken bones for going skydiving, when other people go skydiving without suffering such injuries – and skydiving in normal cases is not morally wrong. And it is not persuasive to maintain that it is a person's fault that he is in pain because he chose the particular surgeon for the particular procedure he had, especially on the supposition that the sufferer in question did prior research and selected the surgeon based on expert recommendations and the surgeon's 99 percent procedural success rate. If the individual turns out to be among the 1 percent, emerging from surgery with a disabling neurological injury, it is not plausible to suppose that he is being punished for his choice to get the needed procedure, which is not wrong, or for some unrelated but sinful act.

Looking around at the world and its inhabitants, we simply do not observe justice in the quality of life or length of life of rational and sentient beings. Some very loving and wonderful people suffer immensely and repeatedly. It is difficult to settle the debate with an opponent who says that the injustices of the world are only apparent injustices and are to be explained by hidden sins in sufferers' lives. The appeal to original sin raises complex problems of its own. It is puzzling as to what evidence could be used to support the hidden sin hypothesis and, on the other side, we cannot prove the nonexistence of secret sins in a person's psyche or moral record, although it does seem that we can plausibly do so with respect to nonhuman animals.

It may be that, as a psychological matter, we tend to take a stance along the lines of the punishment theodicy toward sufferers, including ourselves, as a mechanism of defense against the uncomfortable feeling of being out of control: it is upsetting to think that bad things can happen to good people at any time whatsoever, and naturally one would like to believe that one can acquire and keep good features of one's life if only one behaves correctly and has the right attitudes. As such, a drive for finding out what we have done wrong in order to deserve God's wrath or punishment may, deep down, come from hope – hope for a way out, over which we have some agency. If we just plead in the right way or say the right number of a certain kind of prayer, then maybe God's pleasure with us will be restored and our situation will be lifted. We should take care to notice that adherence to a punishment theodicy can also serve to preserve a sense of self-righteousness on the part of those who do not suffer greatly and as an excuse not to rectify social wrongs.

Still, perhaps we should leave open the theoretical possibility that in some cases of suffering the God-justifying reason for which they are caused or allowed is punishment. But it is not a persuasive line of reasoning for explaining all the evils in the world to say that, in every instance, they are punishments for the sufferers' wrongdoing. It is also not a persuasive suggestion that some victims suffer involuntarily as punishment for the sins of others. Is a beloved child's leukemia supposed to be "what a father gets" for his adultery? Why would a perfect God work that way? I cannot see any good reason that respects the dignity of the child.

3.4 Free Will Theodicy

It is important in thinking through the question of the justification of pain, cruelty, and other evils in relation to theistic belief to acknowledge the significant role played by appeal to the power of human free choice. In Section 3.2, concerning the theodicy according to which suffering in our world is necessary for securing the greater good of providing opportunities for character development through time by way of freely chosen responses to suffering that either degrade or improve the quality of our character, there are underlying issues concerning the nature, existence, and value of human free will. In Section 3.3, as well, concerning the theodicy according to which suffering is divine punishment for wrongdoing, there are underlying issues about the nature, existence, and value of human free will. It makes sense to punish individuals in the sense of retribution only if they are morally responsible for their wrongdoing, and they can be morally responsible for their wrongdoing only if they act wrongly with control over their actions, a control many theorists refer to as free will. We can think of free will as the power to act freely. Many philosophers think that our acting freely is undermined by our being compelled to do what we do by a psychiatric condition, such as kleptomania, and that it is undermined, too, by our being manipulated or forced by another into doing what we do, such as by hypnosis. Some philosophers think that an ability to act freely is also undermined if causal determinism is true, which is the hypothesis that at each moment there is only one way the future can develop, given the laws of nature and the events of the past. Other free agency theorists believe that we can act freely even if causal determinism is true.

According to compatibilist accounts, we can have the power to act freely even if it is true that, at every moment, there is exactly one physically possible future, which is a future consistent with the actual past and the laws of nature. Compatibilists urge us to consider that what undermines agent control over action is *not* the fact, if it is a fact, that every event, including the event of a decision and an action, is brought about by prior causally necessitating events. Rather, what matters to agential freedom is *which* events or kind of events (or states or processes or mechanisms) in particular cause the events of our decisions and other actions.

For instance, on Harry Frankfurt's (1971) influential compatibilist account of free action, a person acts freely when she does what she wants to do and what she wants to want to do. Desires to act Frankfurt calls "first-level desires," and desires to desire to act he calls "second-order desires." Frankfurt's account builds on the natural root idea that we have freedom of action when we are able to act as we want. He observes, though, that not all first-level desires to do things (such as to dance wildly late into the night at a party, neglecting responsibilities to study for an exam and to be well rested for work the next day) reflect, one might say, what we *really* want. Persons, Frankfurt emphasizes, have a remarkable ability for reflective self-evaluation, by way of which we can form desires about our desires themselves. When a person has alignment in the structure of her desires concerning what she does (say, she skips the party and goes to bed on time because she wants to do so and wants to want to do so), with a kind of hierarchical harmony in her psyche, she acts freely, in a way that expresses her true self.

On an alternative compatibilist account set out by Gary Watson (1975), a person acts freely in acting on her values, which are her judgments about what it is good to do in the circumstances that she can defend in a cool and non-self-deceptive moment. Watson later rejected that account on the basis of its being overly rationalistic, but it remains an important account on which we can act freely even if causal determinism is true, since we can act from our values even if we have the values we do because of our genetics and everything that has happened to us over the course of our lives. On John Martin Fischer's compatibilist account of the freedom needed for moral responsibility, a person acts freely in acting from a reasons-responsive mechanism of her own. The notions of reasons-responsiveness, mechanism, and ownership of mechanisms are worked out in Fischer's (2012) work in great detail. On Dana Nelkin's (2011) compatibilist "rational abilities view," an individual is free in performing an action in the sense required for deserved praise and blame if and only if he acts with the ability to recognize and act for good reasons. Susan Wolf's (1990) similar account suggests that a person acts freely when she is able to act in accord with the True and the Good. None of these accounts require the falsity of causal determinism in order for us to act freely.

Now it is a natural move, if one believes in God, to defend the goodness and perfection of God in response to the evils of the world by pointing out that, after all, *God* did not bring about the Holocaust or the Rwandan genocide or a particular sexual assault. Rather, these were caused by human actions – which the theist can suggest, were freely chosen by perpetrators. On the free will theodicy, God remains good and loving, even in light of the suffering in the world, because it is created human beings who freely choose to harm each other and to harm nonhuman animals and the environment. None of this is God's direct doing; the fault is ours, or more precisely the fault of the wrongdoers who use their power of free will to act badly. According to the free will theodicist, it is a great good that God gave us free will and lets us direct the course of our lives largely on our own, by way of our own free choices. With the billions of people on the planet having free will, if we do indeed have it, the result is a whole lot of bad consequences from evil choices, which God is justified in allowing because of the greater good of the gift of free will.

In some cases of suffering, it is true that we can identify the perpetrator, and it is not (at least directly) God, but instead a human being who freely chose to harm someone else: the murderer, or the partner who betrayed the other and broke her heart. But we can think of several problems for this line of thought that puts all the blame for the pain and suffering in the world on the shoulders of the bad free choices of created beings. One problem is that, even in cases of free actions which cause harm to others, if God is there, in control of the universe, then God at least *allows* the harm to be freely done by the perpetrator. Given that God is omnipotent, God could have intervened to prevent the bad choice, or God could have intervened after the choice to prevent its most harmful consequences. God could have made the rapist trip and fall, for instance, preventing the victim's assault. Or God could have made the rapist faint once he started the assault. So why didn't God do that? There must be some good reason. The good of preserving the stability of natural laws is often cited here.

Another problem for the free will theodicy is this: not all cases of suffering are brought about intentionally by human free choices. When there is a bad medical outcome in a surgical case, it is not always the result of someone's malicious intention and not always even the result of professional negligence. Some unsuccessful surgical outcomes simply happen through an unlucky confluence of factors. When lightning strikes a home, no human being freely chose for it to strike that house rather than the neighboring one. When sudden flood waters kill hundreds of people, no human being freely brought this about. (One might say that people freely chose to live in the area and the area is prone to flooding, but where in the world is it perfectly safe to live, and how could we all live is those safe places if there were such places?)

Furthermore, and crucially, the free will appealed to by a free will theodicist also has to be indeterminist (or what is called libertarian) free will, in order for the free will theodicy to be plausible. That is, the free will theodicist has to have in mind an account of human free will which requires that the thesis of causal determinism is false. (For exploration of such accounts, see Ekstrom, 2000, 2019.) He thus has to maintain that the compatibilist accounts of the nature of free agency provided by Frankurt, Watson, Fischer, Nelkin, and Wolf, for example, are inadequate and implausible accounts. In citing the free will of created beings as the greater good that justifies God in permitting instances of

evil or the facts about evil, the free will theodicist who is a theist needs to
maintain, as well, that causal determinism is false, and that we human beings do
have libertarian free will. Without maintaining these positions – the implaus-
ibility of all compatibilist accounts of free agency, the falsity of causal determinism, and the existence of libertarian human freedom – the free will
theodicist has no explanation to offer for the violence and cruelty in the
world, one that shields God and preserves God's goodness, since God could
have set up the initial conditions in the universe and decreed that all events are
governed by deterministic natural laws, so that the unfolding of events in the
world included none that are evil. And God could have done this even in worlds
in which he created free (in a compatibilist sense) rational beings.

If Nelkin has a plausible account of the nature of freedom, for instance, then
God could have made free creatures without there being the evils we find in our
world. On Nelkin's account, for a divine being to make free created beings is to
make beings who can act with an ability to appreciate and to act on good
reasons. Created beings who are free and morally responsible for their actions
would not need an ability to perform a wrong action or the ability to act for bad
reasons. An individual can have the kind of freedom Nelkin depicts even when
all of the decisions and actions available to her are good ones. Likewise, if
Frankfurt's account of free action is right, to have the ability to act freely is to
have the ability to act as one wants to act and as one wants to want to act. God
could create beings who want to act in ways that are good and who want to want
to act in those ways, without failing to grant them freedom or failing to respect
their freedom. Frankfurt's account does not put restrictions on the causal history
of one's desires – it requires for free action only that the first-level and second-
level desires concerning the act in question be in alignment as one acts on them.
Hence, the creation of beings who have freedom, as depicted by the hierarchical
account, need not entail the possibility of evil in the world. Thus, the free will
theodicist must defend the superiority of a libertarian account of freedom in
comparison to compatibilist accounts, and he must defend the claim that we
have libertarian freedom not only with respect to good actions but also with
respect to performing bad actions, even extremely bad ones.

Another problem faces the theodicy according to which God allows suffering
because God wanted to create beings with libertarian free will and God wants to
allow them to carry out their evil intentions, as well as their good ones: such
morally significant (in Alvin Plantinga's terms) libertarian free will – or what
Swinburne calls *serious* free will (libertarian free will with respect to seriously
good and seriously evil potential actions) – has to have *enormous* value, in order
for it to make sense that a perfect being would decide to create beings that have
it. It is difficult to defend the claim that such serious libertarian free will is *worth*

it, that is, is of sufficiently high value to justify the suffering it causes in the world. (I address this issue in detail in Ekstrom, 2021.) If many highly wonderful goods can be secured in worlds where the created beings in them have free will of the sort depicted on any of the various leading compatibilist accounts of free will, without there being evils in those worlds (at all, or in the amounts and intensities we find in our world), and if those worlds are better overall than our world, then a perfect being would have made such a world, instead (or would have elected not to create at all).

This is what I think goes wrong in the perspective of those theists who adopt the stance that, even though God exists, there are pointless evils in the world, and God chose to give human beings free will of a sort that requires causal indeterminism in human free decision making, and God chooses to preserve the stability of natural laws rather than (regularly or intermittently) intervening to prevent bad or the worst outcomes of human free choices, and the future is open, and God is not "meticulously provident" but instead takes risks. Michael Peterson (2022) suggests that this is the right way forward for theists with regard to the problem of evil, and he suggests that this viewpoint does not require the theist to think that this world is somehow overall greater for having the evils that it contains.

As I see it, the theist who adopts this picture on which God grants created human beings libertarian free will and takes risks with the future does imply that the world is overall greater for having the risks of harm (which are evils) and the amount and intensities of evils that it contains, and this is the world, or among the worlds, having the best mixture of goods and evils – or else God is not good and worthy of worship, in virtue of God's deciding to make actual this world or this type of world and *to give us such a power of serious libertarian free choice*. The *risk* of evils is itself *an evil*: it is a vulnerability we rational and sentient creatures have to becoming victims of horrific crimes, such as being shot in school, assaulted, killed through domestic violence, or imprisoned in a concentration camp, and it is a vulnerability we have to suffering as the result of natural disasters. God's electing to create rational and sentient beings with a serious libertarian power of free choice in a naturally indeterministic world has to be a good idea, in order to preserve the perfection of God. Moreover, it has to be a good decision made for justifying reasons, as opposed to God's choosing, instead, to create a different sort of world – such as a world with rational and sentient beings who have a compatibilist power of free choice in a naturally deterministic environment (with less or no evil and yet goods such as joy, peace, health, love, and safety) – or as opposed to creating a world in which there are no sentient beings, and as opposed to not creating anything at all.

4 Theodicies: Divine Intimacy, Relationship-Building, Afterlife, and Atonement

In the previous section, we considered theodicies that cite the goods of contrast between good and evil, appreciation of goodness, divine punishment for human wrongdoing, human soul-making or the temporally extended development of virtuous character traits, and the good of free will. This section delineates and examines additional lines of theodicy.

4.1 Divine Intimacy Theodicy

In this section, and in Section 4.2, we will consider theodicies that emphasize the good of relationship-building. One way of developing the idea emphasizes human relationships with God. In previous work I have called this line of thought a "divine intimacy theodicy" (Ekstrom, 2004). On a divine intimacy theodicy, occasions of suffering allow human beings to experience deepened closeness to God. The core idea is that tragedy, loss, and pain can provide avenues to knowledge of God, such that God is seen or known in the experience of suffering itself. This theodicy is suggested in the work of contemporary philosophers such as Marilyn Adams and Eleonore Stump, as well as in the writings of many Christian mystics of the medieval and later periods (Adams, 1986, 1989, 1999; Stump, 1985, 1994, 1999; see also Wolterstorff, 1988.) The central idea of the divine intimacy theodicy is not the same as John Hick's suggestion that suffering offers us opportunities to improve our moral character – developing traits like courage and patience – but, instead, that through suffering we become closer to God as we become more aware of his loving presence when we are suffering. Perhaps by sharing in God's own suffering if God can suffer, and in our losses, disappointments, and pains, we come to know and rely on God more deeply, becoming more intimate with him in a spiritual way – more full of an awareness of God's existence with us and his love for us.

In the writings of many religious thinkers, we find reports of visions of God and experiences of comfort from God in the midst of suffering. Simone Weil, for example, in a letter to her friend Father Perrin, describes experiences she had while in pain and reciting prayers, when, she says, God "came down and took possession of me ... I only felt in the midst of my suffering the presence of a love, like that which one can read in the smile on a beloved face" (Weil, 1951). Julian of Norwich likewise reports a divine vision while in the midst of suffering a severe illness for which she had received last rites: "At once I saw the red blood trickling down under the garland, hot, fresh, and plentiful, just as it did at the time of his passion when the crown of thorns was pressed on to the blessed head of God-and-Man .... And I had a strong, deep, conviction that it was he himself" (Julian of Norwich, 1984, p. 66). She recounts that, in her suffering, she perceived God: "I saw that he is to us everything which is good and comforting for our help. He is our clothing, who wraps and enfolds us for love, embraces us and shelters us, surrounds us for his love." (Julian of Norwich, Long Text 5 [c. 1400], quoted in Flinders, 1993, p. 88). Many individuals in sorrow and pain have similarly reported a vision of the divine or a feeling of God's nearness and comfort in their distress. In the account of Job, while suffering tremendous losses and physical distress, he utters to God, "My ears had heard of you but now my eyes have seen you" (Job 42:5). In his suffering, Job recounts, he has met God – God has shown himself to the sufferer. In contemporary philosophy of religion, too, we find the suggestion that the most profound religious experiences some individuals have come when they are in deep sorrow, pain, or grief. Nicholas Wolterstorff, for instance, writes hauntingly about his experience of wrestling with the question of why God would have allowed his young adult son to have fallen to his death while climbing, in the prime of his life, stealing someone who was deeply loved and central to his family's identity and joy. "Through the prism of my tears," Wolsterstorff writes, "I have seen a suffering God" (Wolsterstorff, 1987, pp. 80–81).

Some religious thinkers reject the idea that God suffers, largely because they take impassibility to be an implication of God's immutability. Regardless of where one stands on that matter, a theist in the Christian tradition, in particular, might view occasions of enduring rejection, pain, and loss as opportunities for identification with the person of Jesus Christ, such that suffering provides deeper appreciation of his passion. Marilyn Adams suggests that instances of suffering, even horrendous ones, might be made meaningful by being integrated into the sufferer's relationship with God through identification with Christ, understood either as sympathetic identification (in which each person suffers his own pain, enabling the human sufferer to know what it is like for Christ) or as mystical identification (in which the human sufferer literally experiences a share of Christ's pain). Alternately, Adams suggests, meaningfulness may derive from suffering serving as a vision into the inner life of God, either because God is not impassible, or because the sheer intensity of the experience gives one a glimpse of what it is like to be beyond joy and sorrow (Adams, 1989, 1999).

A divine intimacy theodicy may be available from the perspective of other religious traditions, as well. Michael J. Harris focuses on a rabbinic concept discussed in the Talmud Bavli (at *Berakhot* 5a–b) of *yissurin shel ahavah*, "the sufferings (or "afflictions") of love," suggesting that *yissurin shel ahavah* is most compellingly construed as a divine intimacy theodicy, rather than as a punishment theodicy or a soul-making theodicy. Harris surveys significant rabbinic writers who have understood the idea in this way, including Talmudic and other important later sources. He writes that, moreover, "the idea that suffering can be productive of intimacy with God is ... found in Jewish sources even independently of *yissurin shel ahavah* .... . It would seem that divine intimacy theodicy is not just an interesting notion for Christian thinkers but is worthy of consideration as part of a traditional Jewish theological approach to the problem of suffering" (Harris, 2016, pp. 64–92.).

In sum, the suggestion of the divine intimacy theodicy is that God allows us to suffer because this enables us to share in experience of God himself and enables persons vividly to experience God's presence and love, developing closeness between the sufferer and God. In these ways, suffering could contribute positively to an individual's relationship with God.

One objection to the divine intimacy theodicy is a concern about futility or ineffectiveness. Very common reactions to suffering include confusion, bitterness, and rejection of God's existence, rather than a sense of closeness to God. Suffering, we must acknowledge, is often experienced without feeling a presence of a loving God and, in fact, can be accompanied by a vivid impression that God does not exist. When ill or deeply sad or devastated by loss, we may feel utterly alone, as if no one cares, and we do not feel comforted by a perfect being who supposedly permitted us to suffer as we do in order for us to become close to him. The divine intimacy theodicist might reply to this observation by pointing out that it does not follow from the fact that some persons reject God through their suffering, or do not feel God's loving presence, that occasions of suffering do not provide opportunities for intimacy with God. It could be that God is present and available to support a person who chooses not to acknowledge that this is so, and one might be sharing in the experience of God who suffers, without one's being appreciative of this fact.

How should one assess the overall plausibility of the divine intimacy theodicy? One important point is this: the appeal to the idea that occasions of suffering offer an opportunity for intimacy with God rather than a guarantee, shows, again – like the retributive punishment theodicy, free will theodicy, and character-building theodicy – a reliance on the existence and positive value of libertarian human free choice. Compatibilist free will does not turn the trick, as we saw in the previous section, since God could have actualized a world in which created persons have such free will (for instance, the ability to act on hierarchically aligned desires) without the facts about evil we observe in our world – concerning amount, intensity, and distribution – being what they are. A divine intimacy theodicist who wants to accommodate certain cases of suffering by postulating that, in permitting those instances of suffering, God offers the great good of an opportunity for the sufferer to achieve new or deeper intimacy with God, but the sufferer freely failed to take advantage of the opportunity (so that the nonachievement of the justifying good is not God's fault), will need to rely on the existence and positive value of libertarian free will.

A second point is the recognition that intimacy with God is not available to every being who suffers. I think in the end it has to be admitted that the divine intimacy theodicy can provide at most a very partial justificatory account. The view simply cannot plausibly cover all of the facts about evil in our world. Most prominent among the problem cases are those involving the suffering of nonhuman animals: it seems quite unlikely that the pain endured by all sentient nonhuman animals by way of neglect, abuse, torture, disease, and natural disaster can be justified by connection with, or intimacy with, God. The widespread instances of suffering of infants and very young children, too – some born into deep poverty and deprivation, some with debilitating illnesses, some who die slow, wasting deaths from starvation, some who are maliciously abused – frankly are not credibly claimed to be covered by the divine intimacy theodicy. Even if, in such cases, the sufferers were capable of intimacy with God, it is hard to maintain the goodness of God alongside the claim that such cases of suffering are necessary for the individuals who suffer to be close to God. Why would God not show his existence and love in better ways, or create beings who are full of a joyful, loving, direct acquaintance with God without their enduring tortures and pain? In sum, despite the use it might have in suggesting means by which a theist might cope in the midst of suffering, the divine intimacy theodicy ultimately comes up short as a response to the arguments from evil in Sections 1 and 2.

4.2 Relationship-Building Theodicy

This section describes a somewhat different theodicy based in relationship-building. A related line of thinking to the divine intimacy theodicy is that God allows suffering so that we can better bond with, and become closer to, other created beings, including nonhuman animals and other human persons. In hunger and poverty, and pain and loss and illness, we become more aware of our shared humanity and our shared sentience. We strengthen our sense of community. It is suffering that "brings us together," as when a natural disaster destroys property, but people come together to help each other rebuild (see Collins, 2013). There is no doubt that shared hardship and loss do forge bonds between people. And our bonds with others are strengthened when we listen to them when they are in pain, when we sit with them in empathy, and when we do what we can to ease their burdens and help them gain improved functioning in life. We feel closer to people who listen to us when we are in grief or ill, people who do not judge us but who show that they care and genuinely try to understand, and who take delight in us and our presence together, even as we suffer. Some of the best moments in life, one might say, come in being deeply understood and in deeply understanding someone else, and often it is some kind of suffering or loss that makes this kind of empathetic connection possible. Many nonhuman animals, too, show capacities for empathy and care and efforts at help and support for one another. In short, pain and evils of various kinds can enable relationship-building.

Can the good of relationship-building work as a justifying reason for God to cause or permit the cases of suffering we observe in the world? The relationship-building theodicist will need to identify cases in which the strength and goodness of relationships developed by the suffering were worth it as an outweighing good and were a good for which the suffering was necessary – that is, cases in which the good of relationship closeness could not have been brought about in any other or better way. If you could have become just as close to your new friend by sharing a love of jazz music as you did by sharing the experience of pudendal neuralgia, then the suffering and disability you each endure from pudendal neuralgia cannot be justified by its being necessary for bringing about the good of your close friendship. Similarly, if a girl sold into sexual slavery could have been just as filled with a sense of the presence and love of her sister in walking through the great art museums of the world as she is through her horrific pain and abuse, then that pain and abuse cannot be justified by their being necessary for her development of closeness with her sister.

On their most plausible versions, the relationship-building theodicies, including the divine intimacy theodicy, depend on the existence and high value of human free will. This is because it is clear that not everyone becomes closer to others (or closer to God) through suffering. Some people become bitter, isolated, mistrusting, and distant from others as a result of the ways in which they have suffered, often at the hands of others. The relationship-building theodicies are thus best defended as proposing the good of offering opportunities for developing closeness to God or closeness to other persons or nonhuman animals, opportunities which may or may not be freely taken.

Like the character-building theodicy and the divine intimacy theodicy, the relationship-building theodicy seems limited in scope, leaving out wide swaths of cases, including infants and toddlers who die prematurely and the vast amount of nonhuman animal suffering.

4.3 Appeal to the Afterlife

It is a natural thought for theists that, if we are trying to identify goods that might justify God in permitting the evils of the world, we should not be confined to goods found only in the earthly lives of rational and sentient beings. Our lives on Earth are rather short from a broader perspective that includes the history and future of the universe, and the goods that justify God in permitting the evils we endure during our life spans, whether they be of 35 or 96 or 12 or even 105 years, might well be goods that exist beyond that limited time frame. Indeed, we have already considered appeal to the goods of growing intimacy with God, loving relationship with God, and mutually supporting, empathetic relationships with other rational and sentient beings – and these might well extend, a theodicist may suggest, into an afterlife.

Depending on one's views about what God can do with respect to preserving our identity and views about the nature of existing rational and sentient beings – whether or not we have an immaterial soul, for instance, or whether or not God might be able to take purely physical beings who die on Earth and somehow reconstruct or reform them in such a way that they continue to live in another state or type of existence – the idea that there is an afterlife might seem more or less plausible. We might grant that we do not know for certain that there is not an afterlife, and that it is logically possible that the lives of some or all rational and sentient creatures extend beyond the earthly grave. In a number of religious traditions, there is an afterlife existence that involves eternal joy and freedom from suffering, ecstatic union with the Creator of the universe, or deep and abiding love in the presence of God. Recent polling suggests that 73 percent of US adults believe in heaven (78 percent of women and 68 percent of men) (Pew Research Center, 2021). Among those who identify as Christian, 92 percent believe in heaven. When asked about characteristics of heavenly existence, 69 percent of respondents said that people are probably or definitely free from suffering, 65 percent said that in heaven individuals are reunited with loved ones who have previously died, and 62 percent said that we can meet God.

If, after earthly death, persons in heaven can be in the presence of God and perhaps, too, enjoy continued loving and joyful relationships with other persons, then the sheer enormity and depth of joy, love, and bliss experienced in this afterlife – which one may suggest continues for all eternity – would so far surpass in goodness all that we have experienced in our earthly lives that the experiences of these lives we are living, here and now, might be viewed as rather pale and unimportant. It is true that what we suffer while on Earth is finite in duration. The theodicist who appeals to afterlife goods might say that these finitely endured periods of suffering are overwhelmed and swamped by the indescribably great good of heavenly existence of infinite length. Stephen Maitzen (2009) refers to a line of thought like this as a "Heaven Swamps Everything" theodicy.

There are different ways in which one might fill in an afterlife theodicy. One might suggest that, from the perspective of heaven, a person will not care any longer about what she endured on Earth, or it will seem trivial to her. Or one might suggest that, in heaven, a person will not complain about her pains, disappointments, and losses during earthly life, given her state of eternal bliss in the presence of God, or that she will have forgotten about what she endured. Alternatively, one might suggest that, although she remembers her suffering, she will forgive the agents of her suffering. Or one might suggest that she will see her earthly sufferings as simply overwhelmed by the great goodness of heavenly existence, which serves as compensation for them. The afterlife theodicist might suggest that several of these ideas are true, the central point being that heavenly existence is such a surpassingly great good that earthly pains are, in the scope of things, insignificant, and they are compensated for by God in an eternal heavenly experience after earthly death.

Notice that the afterlife theodicist must be careful: if she says that, in light of heaven, our earthly pains are nothing, one can rightly reply that, taken literally, this statement is patently false: rape is not nothing; the loss of one's child to a devastating disease is not nothing; and the endurance of persistent neuropathic pain over the span of seventy years is not nothing. Such pains, losses, and assaults are real, and even if there is a heavenly afterlife, the individuals who endure rape, the death of a child, and chronic pain while they live on earth do indeed experience devastating suffering. The question remains concerning what justifies God in causing or allowing such experiences of suffering by individuals God loves. As Maitzen points out, and as we can clearly appreciate, compensation is not justification. An abusive husband who gives his wife an emerald ring after a particularly violent abusive episode toward her does not provide any justification for what he did to her, and he does not thereby give an explanation or an apology, but merely tries to compensate her in some way, to attempt somehow to make up for what he put her through. Likewise, if you attack and injure someone and then later give him a thousand dollars, you have not justified your attack but have merely offered compensation.

God's providing a person with eternal bliss or union with God in an afterlife is obviously not lame or crass, as are the giving of the ring and the money, and one might suggest that to use such analogies is to underappreciate the surpassing and transcendent good of heaven. However, the key point is this: to count as such, a theodicy must offer a *justifying reason* for which God causes or allows suffering. If one person endures sexual assault and another does not, and both end up in heaven, it is fair to ask why God allowed the first to be assaulted but spared the second, and why God elects to create a universe in which sexual assaults take place at all. To say that sufferers later forgive those who harmed them, or that they forget about the negative experiences they endured, or that they no longer care in the light of heaven, is not to offer an explanation or justification for why God permitted individuals to suffer during their earthly lives as they did.

Now the afterlife theodicist might say something along the lines that Maitzen suggests in spelling out the Heaven Swamps Everything theodicy: the idea is that "compensation paid to an exploited human being somehow *becomes* justification for the exploitation if the compensation is big enough" – as it is in the case of eternal bliss. However, this suggestion is at odds with our moral compass. As Maitzen rightly counters, "such reasoning wars with ordinary morality because it *conflates* compensation and justification" (Maitzen, 2009, pp. 122–123). One might try to improve the afterlife theodicy by suggesting that, in the afterlife, victims of suffering on Earth receive divine gratitude for their endurance and their persistent faith through earthly suffering (Adams 1999; Plantinga 2004). But, again, this offers only compensation afterward with divine gratitude, not justification for permitting the suffering in the first place. The afterlife theodicist might again emphasize that, in heaven, individuals are in an ecstatic state of mind. Still, as Maitzen points out, "our ordinary moral practice recognizes a legitimate complaint about child abuse even if, as adults, its victims should happen to be on drugs that make them uninterested in complaining" (Maitzen, 2009, p. 123).

Consider a line of theodicy that appeals to the afterlife recently sketched by Timothy O'Connor (forthcoming). He writes:

> He [God] might well deploy a very long and complex process that involves unequally distributed difficulty, distress, shockwaves of pain, physical debilitation, psychological fragmentation, and, yes, outright horror – *if* He deems that torturous path through evil to *constitutively contribute* to a work of tremendous and terrible moral and aesthetic beauty .... [This process] will culminate not merely in great and lasting *individual* goods, but also (if Christian teaching be true) *transtemporal, communal* goods: the fulfillment of divine promises originally made to generations who hoped for but never saw them; deeper communal understanding of what the love of God calls us to that is achieved through difficulties and failures across generations and disparate cultures ... and the shared joy and mutual love of the redeemed as they experience full union with God, making them *collectively* more perfect icons of the inter-penetrating love of the triune God.

It is helpful that O'Connor gestures toward a theodicy of "individuals making asymmetrical contributions" to the "collective goods" of a diverse community, culminating in "shared joy and mutual love of the redeemed as they experience full union with God" in heaven, in virtue of providing a proposal, but in my view the picture he offers violates an appropriate victim-centered constraint on successful theodicy. It is reasonable to hold that a perfectly good agent would not use an intrinsically valuable rational and sentient being *as a means* for the good of someone else or for a communal end (let alone for aesthetic beauty) and that, instead, God would respect us as ends in ourselves. When O'Connor writes (in this same piece) that, "Theodicy worthy of the name would require deep insight into the life to come, both the individual and profoundly communal aspects of the ecstatic experience of union with the Author of life," I wonder if this is suggesting that for all we know the suffering of this world is *all* needed – in its amount, intensity, and inequitable distribution – and each instance is needed for the best communal afterlife experience of ecstasy. It is natural to ask: How is a particular girl's life in sexual slavery in Southeast Asia required for our *communal afterlife ecstasy*? How is another girl's (and many girls') gang rape and physical mutilation, causing oozing fistulas in the Democratic Republic of the Congo, and other places, necessary for the communal ecstatic union with the Author of life?

Again, in any plausible theodicy, the harm must be *necessary for* the benefit. And as Eleonore Stump expresses the victim-centered constraint on plausible theodicy, "if a good God allows evil, it can only be because the evil in question produces a benefit for the sufferer and one that God could not produce without the suffering"(Stump, 1985, pp. 411–413). Jeff Jordan (2004) advises that theists should reject constraints like this one, including the principle that God permits undeserved, involuntary human suffering only if such suffering ultimately produces a net benefit for the sufferer. But even if we were to reject a victim-centered constraint, which I do not think there is good reason to do, there remains the point that, if we want to bring about something good but know that it will harm someone who is innocent in the process, we should at least ask their permission; if they consent, knowing about an offered compensation, then perhaps their agreement to our plan helps to justify our act, provided the harm is *necessary for* the end and the end is sufficiently good. But to go ahead without asking is to use them as a means to our end, and if God has brought about a world in which evil is unfairly distributed and this unfair distribution is somehow necessary for some greater communal good, then God has used persons without their consent as a means to whatever that end is – even if they receive compensation in the afterlife. A heavenly afterlife might bring us rest and relief from the evils we suffered while on Earth, and even joy greater than we can currently envision. But we certainly hurt as we suffer here and now, in many cases horrifically and intensely, and a positive afterlife experience does not offer a moral justification for why a perfect God could permit such evils in the first place. The fact that evils are finite does not imply that they did not exist, or that they were not painful or horrific or devastating while endured. In short, even if heaven "swamps" everything horrid that happens during the earthly lives of rational and sentient beings, it does not thereby justify it.

Notice, as well, that the problem of hell complicates a theodicy that appeals to goods in the afterlife. In the Pew Research Center (2021) poll cited earlier, 62 percent of US adults reported believing in hell (79 percent of Christians). Arguably, the view on which some persons spend an eternity suffering in hell generates a particularly virulent argument from evil (Lewis 2007; Ekstrom 2021). An afterlife theodicy according to which *all* persons go to heaven might provide hope to a theist for a time when all suffering ends and all individuals experience surpassing joy, but it does not provide justifying reasons for God's permitting each instance of evil in our world to occur and for making a world like this one in which the facts of evil are what they are. Given its reliance on the existence of an unobserved afterlife, this theodicy is also not useful in moving a nontheist to deny the key premises in the arguments from evil.

4.4 Incarnation and Atonement

In Christian thinking about the problem of evil, there is available a line of theodicy which highlights the divine taking on of human form – incarnation – and suffering death by crucifixion as punishment for the sins of humanity (and subsequent rising from the dead) – atonement. In his paper, "Surpalapsarianism, or 'O Felix Culpa'," Alvin Plantinga suggests that divine incarnation and atonement are a "towering and magnificent good" (Plantinga, 2004, p. 9) and that God's ultimate aim is to create a world of a certain level of value, which "requires that he aim to create a world in which there is incarnation and atonement – which, in turn, requires that there be sin and evil" (Plantinga, 2004, p. 12). Referring to happy fault or the fortunate (or blessed) fall of humanity into sin, Plantinga suggests that "the Felix Culpa approach can perhaps provide us with a theodicy" (Plantinga, 2004, p. 14) The theodicy's suggestion is that suffering and evil in our world are justified in virtue of their being necessary for the towering good of salvation by way of incarnation and atonement. In the course of developing the theodicy, Plantinga articulates a striking value claim:

> Contrast two kinds of possible worlds. In the first kind, there are free creatures who always do only what is right, who live in love and harmony with God and each other, and do so, let's add, through all eternity. Now for each of these worlds W of this kind, there is a world W* of the second kind. In W* God creates the very same creatures as in W; but in W* these free

creatures rebel against him, fall into sin and wickedness, turn their backs upon God. In W*, however, God graciously provides a means of salvation by way of incarnation and atonement. My claim is that for any such worlds W and W*, W* is a better world than W. (Plantinga, 2004, pp. 10–11)

Plantinga calls this the moderate value assumption and says that, although he is inclined to accept it and an even stronger value assumption, his argument only requires the weaker value assumption that "all the worlds in which incarnation and atonement are present are worlds of very great goodness, achieving that level L of goodness such that no world without incarnation and atonement achieves that level" (Plantinga, 2004, p. 11). So if God wants to make actual a possible world the value of which exceeds L, God will create a world containing incarnation and atonement. In answer to the question, *why does God permit evil?*, Plantinga, then, writes, "because he wanted to actualize a possible world whose value was greater than L; but all those possible worlds contain incarnation and atonement; hence all those worlds contain evil. So ... what we have here is a theodicy – and, if I'm right, a successful theodicy" (Plantinga, 2004, p. 12).

Notice in the statement of the moderate value assumption excerpted above, Plantinga grants that it is logically possible for there to be "free creatures who do only what is right, who live in love and harmony with God and each other" for all eternity. This grants that love for God does not require serious morally significant libertarian free will, and love for other persons does not require serious morally significant libertarian free will, and created free beings' living in harmony with God for eternity does not require serious morally significant libertarian free will. This admission poses problems for those theodicists who want to defend the value of serious morally significant free will by appeal to its (alleged) necessity for love of God, necessity for love among created beings, and necessity for afterlife union with God. Plantinga adds to the central idea of the Felix Culpa theodicy, namely, the idea that evil and suffering are justified by their necessity for divine incarnation and atonement, the value claim that "free creatures come in a variety of versions, and not all free creatures are equal with respect to value" (Plantinga, 2004, p. 15). In particular, he contends, "creatures that have a great deal of power, including power to do both good and evil, are more valuable than creatures who are free, but whose power is limited or meager" (Plantinga, 2004, p. 15).

It is not clear what grounds that value claim – that it is a greater gift for God to give created beings a freedom that includes the ability to "turn their backs upon God, to rebel against him, fight against what he values" (Plantinga, 2004, p. 15) than it is to give them freedom as characterized by the rational abilities account (the ability to do the right thing from an appreciation of right reasons, requiring no evil) or the hierarchical account (the ability to do what one wants to do and wants to want to do, requiring no evil) – if that value claim about freedom is meant to be defensible apart from appeal to divine atonement. In the previous sentence, I have left out "incarnation and" in Plantinga's Felix Culpa theodicy's appeal to the good of divine incarnation and atonement: this is because God could become incarnate should God wish to in worlds that contain no freely chosen wrongdoing or suffering at all. It is atonement that requires freely chosen wrongdoing, by the very nature of atonement: there would be no need for atonement if there were not wrongdoing as a response to which atonement is called for. Plantinga writes that it is through Christ's suffering "that he atones for human sin and enables human beings to achieve union with God"(Plantinga, 2004, p. 18). But since he has admitted above that created beings could live in love and harmony with God and others for eternity without having a power ever to do anything wrong, he needs to hold, as he does, that "by virtue of our fall and subsequent redemption, we can achieve a level of intimacy with God that can't be achieved in any other way" (Plantinga, 2004, p. 18). In other words, it is a crucial aspect of the Felix Culpa theodicy that "the final condition of human beings, in this world, is better than it is in the worlds in which there is no fall into sin but also no incarnation and redemption" (Plantinga, 2004, p. 25). As Plantinga spells out that better final condition, "they receive God's thanks, enjoy a greater intimacy with him, are invited to join that charmed circle [of the Trinity]" (Plantinga, 2004, p. 25). The plausibility of the Felix Culpa theodicy depends upon one's assessment of the theodicy's core value claims in relation to the instances of evil in our world and the facts about evil in our world.

4.5 Hybrid Theodicy and Summation

Perhaps a theist could mount a hybrid theodicy, suggesting that some instances of suffering are punishment for wrongdoing, others offer opportunities for character development, others offer opportunities for experiencing closeness with God, others are permitted for the good of opportunities to build human relationships, others are necessary for a person's admission to a heavenly afterlife, and others are a result of serious morally significant libertarian free will and original sin, which God permitted for the great good of there being divine atonement. I think this strategy fails for reasons given above (Section 1.4) in support of the premise that there are pointless evils in the world, and for reasons given above (Section 2.3) in support of the first premise of the argument from the facts about evil.

It is important to assess carefully the proposed justifications for suffering in relation to God that we have examined over the course of this and the previous section. It is also important to notice that these ways of thinking can cause harm.

It adds insult to injury for someone in persistent pain, for instance, to be told that "Everything happens for a reason" or "God never gives us more than we can handle" or "God chose you for this pain journey" or "You need to forgive someone in order to be released from your pain." Some theodicies blame people for their own suffering – such as the punishment theodicy – while others encourage us to find other people to blame for our pain – such as the free will theodicy, in its focus on human rather than divine wrongdoing – and others imply that we do not have good character traits and are being "refined" or given opportunities to grow in virtue as we suffer – such as the soul-making theodicy. The idea that we suffer so that others may develop into more compassionate people, or so that there is greater communal afterlife ecstasy, does not explain how God, in allowing us to be used in this way, could be treating us with dignity and respect and not only as means. When we judge other people who are in persistent pain or poverty as at fault, thinking they must be doing something wrong or else God would not allow them to suffer in the ways they do, we are setting ourselves above them as if we are morally superior, which is not only rationally suspect but also cruel. When we fail to recognize the extent to which all of us human beings are vulnerable to accident, injury, disease, and disability at any moment, we lack humility and a proper sense of commonality.

In sum, when we are suffering ourselves, and as we live in the midst of human and nonhuman animal suffering on a vast scale, we should take care in how we explain our own and others' pain and distress in relation to God. There simply seem to be instances of suffering for which there is no point. The sexual assault and murder of children provide examples, as do repeated instances of different kinds of suffering in one person's life, such as the fourth time a kind and loving mother's back disk herniates, leaving her unable to work and to care for her children, after she has already endured domestic violence and additional cruelties and losses. These cases are not fictitious – some people get visited and revisited with pain and suffering of the same kind or different kinds throughout their lifetimes, including the lightning strike that sets fire to the house, for the second time, of a man who is already paralyzed from contracting polio as a child and who has suffered years of pain, disability, and loneliness. We must acknowledge, too, the large-scale horrendous suffering of slavery and genocide, and the appallingly high incidence of intractable pain. We have not identified a convincing reason or set of reasons that could justify a perfect God in causing or allowing such suffering.

5 Making Meaning

This final section serves as a bridge between theoretical treatments of evil in relation to God and the practical problem of living in a world filled with suffering. It describes the project of making meaning, as opposed to the project of theodicy. The first is a matter of gaining insight and guidance for living with luck, pointless suffering, and theologically unjustified facts about suffering, in contrast to providing justifying reasons for instances of, and the facts about, suffering in defense of the rationality of theism. With respect to meaning in life, the section describes Leo Tolstoy's struggle to find purpose, which ends in faith in God, as well as Susan Wolf's reflections on meaning in life. My own account of making meaning out of suffering is set out. I suggest that life can be meaningful without our making meaning out of our suffering, and suffering can be accepted as simply pointless without undermining one's living a life that is richly meaningful and fulfilling. Still I suggest that, even if the prospects for the project of theodicy are dim with respect to defending the rationality of theistic belief in light of suffering, nonetheless, work in theodicies is useful, and theistic belief itself might be pragmatically justified.

5.1 Meaning in Life

In approaching the topic of meaning in human life, we might follow the lead of Richard Taylor, who in an intriguing essay (Taylor, 1970) begins by noting that, since the notion of a meaningful life is a difficult one on which to get a grasp, it might help to begin with the picture in mind of a life that is meaningless. Taylor chooses the case of Sisyphus, who is condemned by the gods to push a large boulder up a hill, only to have it roll back down again, day after day in a continuing cycle, with all of his toil never amounting to anything at all. Taylor suggests, somewhat surprisingly, that even if we changed the story of Sisyphus to imagine that the boulders do make it to the top of the hill and together are used to form a cathedral, still, we have not constructed an image of a meaningful life. Why? Because, Taylor suggests, once Sisyphus's cathedral is finished, he will have nothing to do but to stare at it, completed, feeling utter boredom – the daily rolling process, which had structured his days, will be over. Having our projects "amount to something" does not provide meaning, Taylor suggests, and anyway everything on Earth eventually crumbles and fades away to nothingness in the long stretch of time. A natural reading of Taylor's (1970) essay is as suggesting that there is no objective overarching meaning or purpose to human life apart from biological survival and reproduction – "the meaning of life is simply to be living, in the manner in which it is your nature to live," he writes – yet that perhaps we can find subjective meaning in what we do by wanting to do what we do, by finding in ourselves a drive for our activities and projects.

Does doing anything at all we find in ourselves a drive or desire to do, though, make for meaning in life? Certain cases provide challenges to such a proposal, such as a person's leaving a professional life involved in education, scholarly research, and writing, to stay at home, lining up rows of colored jelly beans, all day every day, even with a desire to do so.

Susan Wolf's insightful works on meaning in life (Wolf, 2007, 2010) provide a framework for analyzing such cases. From Wolf's perspective, there is no overarching purpose to human existence unless there is a God who created us for a purpose – which she does not think there is – but, still, whether or not our individual lives have meaning in them is something that is up to us. We can make a distinction between the question of the meaning of life, as in the purpose for human existence as a whole – in other words, why, in a purposive and perhaps explanatory sense we, collectively, are here – on the one hand, and meaningfulness in our individual lives, on the other. Wolf describes individuals' lives as having meaning in them when they are actively engaged in projects of positive value with some measure of success (Wolf, 2007). Her view incorporates subjective elements of active intentional engagement, as opposed to passivity and disinterest, as well as objective elements, in virtue of requiring that the projects structuring a meaningful life have, in fact, positive value. This account rules out, as meaningful, lives that are engaged in sheer busyness for the sake of busyness not directed at any particular valuable end, such as, in the case above, spending one's days lining up colored candies (not as an artistic production, but only for pleasure or mindlessly to pass the time). In her book, Wolf (2010) puts this account of meaning in life in somewhat different terms: we lead meaningful lives when we love what is worth loving. This formulation also captures the hybrid of subjective and objective elements: our loves must be *worth loving* and we must *actively love* what we love, if we are to live meaningful lives. The insufficiency of either element alone is indicated by the phenomenon of waking up to the realization that one's life has been lacking in meaning. In so waking up, one realizes that one has been too passive and unengaged, not really loving anything at all, or that one has been actively engaged in projects that lack positive value.

In conducting lives that have meaning, on this account, the projects in which we actively engage ourselves need not be projects that are morally good, although they might be: working to feed those who are starving, for instance, may provide meaning in a person's life, as may assisting in the project of providing education in areas of the world where educational access has been lacking or to populations that are economically and socially underprivileged. Wolf emphasizes that other, nonmoral, projects have positive value as well: artistic projects, for example, and the development of athletic skill and culinary excellence. These, too, can be worth loving. Wolf's account can capture the sense some individuals have that their lives have meaning in virtue of being a part of something larger than themselves, such as playing a role in working to make society more just and equitable, or taking part in a collective medical endeavor to develop effective vaccines for emerging viral infections, or being a professional member of a theatre company dedicated to artistic excellence. Being actively engaged in such positively valuable projects makes for meaning in life.

5.2 Making Meaning out of Suffering

I think we can usefully apply this work on meaning in life to our experiences of coping with evils such as loss, injustice, and persistent pain, as well as to our care for other human beings (and nonhuman animals) who are suffering. To take the latter first, when we help other human beings who are in pain to cope – when we do what we can to ameliorate their situations, by arranging their medical appointments, accompanying them to their consultations and procedures, cooking meals for them, keeping them company, telling them amusing stories or, in the case of (some) nonhuman animals, adopting them and providing loving care – these are surely ways of being actively engaged in projects that have positive value: namely, the project of helping someone who is in pain of any sort to endure and persist, and to seek whatever treatment may be available or whatever social service might assist. As actively engaged caregivers to loved ones, community members, and friends, we live out the positively valuable project of providing love, emotional support, physical help, and advocacy for people who are suffering, whether in grief, tragedy, or persistent pain. We can do the same for some nonhuman animals, including by protecting habitats, and we can contribute to helping ameliorate the suffering of human beings who are strangers to us across the globe by offering our resources of time, energy, and funds, as we are able. These are surely meaningful forms of human life.

When we ourselves are the ones who are suffering, whether in emotional pain from betrayal or loss or injustice, or in intense or lasting physical pain of some kind, how do we make meaning of our pain or construct meaningful lives while suffering, even while in in the midst of it? We might separate two questions here. One is the question, how do we create meaningful lives *despite* our being in a state of deep mourning or other emotional suffering or in persistent physical pain? And a second question is, how do we make meaning *out of our pain and suffering*? The second is a question about how we might make sense of our suffering, how we might find the condition itself meaningful or in the service of some purpose.

We have considered various proposed theodicies, attempts at providing God-justifying reasons for causing or allowing the suffering we find in our world. I argued that it is unreasonable to think regarding every sufferer on Earth, human and nonhuman, that their afflictions were sent to them directly by God, or permitted by a God who could have stopped their afflictions but chose not to. The conclusion that is most rational to reach, from my perspective, is this: it is a horrible shame that we suffer, and many of us suffer in the ways we do by way of a variety of causal factors that all sum up to count as a matter of very bad luck. If this is correct and it is a matter of *very bad luck* that anyone suffers, for instance, with a painful disability or an incurable disease or as the victim of a sexual assault, then can there be any meaning in it, in the suffering itself?

One suggestion is that we can make meaning out of suffering ourselves if we choose to, by using our pain to motivate us to become actively engaged in projects related to our suffering that are positively valuable projects. We could build on Wolf's insights about meaningful lives in different ways. For instance, we can make meaning out of our suffering by working to help others who cope with pain. We might serve as a volunteer at a local hospital or a hospice, or we might go out of our way to encourage friends, family members, neighbors, and colleagues when we learn that they are in distress, or we might start a support group in person or online for people who endure protracted illness or disability, or we might write a book about suffering. In these ways, we can use our own pain as motivation for actively engaging ourselves in a worthwhile project that involves helping others who, like us, live with pain and suffering.

But we do not have to do something that helps others to cope with pain and suffering in order for us to build meaningful lives while we are in pain. We do not have to, in other words, make meaning out of our pain or trauma. We could take a cue from Wolf's account in a different way: we can actively engage ourselves in projects that are positively valuable, without those projects being centered on helping sufferers. That is, there is nothing about meaning in life that requires that, because we suffer pain, we must help others who are in pain in order to live meaningful lives. We can have meaningful lives by engaging ourselves as actively as is possible for us in any number of positively valuable projects, including raising children, developing artistic talents, making a career in computing or law or contracting or administration or plumbing or science or hospitality, and so on. There are very many ways to actively engage ourselves in undertakings that do matter, in projects that have positive value. We can create meaning in our lives despite our pain or trauma, without the meaning in our lives centering on pain or trauma.

5.3 How Theodicies Are Useful

We can also take cues from some of the lines of theodicy discussed in Sections 3 and 4 as practical advice for living in a pain-filled world. I do not see comfort or advice in the theodicy on which we suffer as divine punishment for what we or others have done wrong. However, we can look to the goods highlighted in other lines of thought. For example, loving, caring, and mutually supporting human relationships are great sources of joy and comfort, as well as potential sources of self-understanding, empathy, and personal and intellectual growth. We can treasure our human relationships, nurture them, and enjoy them. In addition, the character-development theodicy emphasizes the good of becoming more virtuous through time. Given that we suffer, we can also use our suffering to build patience, compassion, and persistence. We can respond to the suffering of others by becoming more generous and kind. The free will theodicy's emphasis on the good of human freedom can guide us toward thinking about the powers we have as agents to plan, to direct our thoughts, and to consider and act upon reasons, exercising control over what we can.

Divine intimacy theodicies might help us to feel a sense of comfort and camaraderie if we envision ourselves as accompanied in our suffering by a divine being who perhaps is not absolutely perfect but who lacks the power to prevent our suffering and who grieves with and strengthens us as we endure (see Kushner 1981). An afterlife theodicy might direct our thoughts forward in time, offering us hope for a time in the future, whether after earthly death when we are pain-free either because nonexistent or because in some heavenly type of experience, or a time later in earthly life when our suffering may be less than it is in the present. An incarnation and atonement theodicy might not be one we take to be theoretically successful, but nonetheless it might prompt us to be grateful for those who love us and who sacrifice their own interests to help and care for us.

5.4 Pragmatic Justification of Religious Belief

Tolstoy (2008) recounts a time of personal crisis regarding the meaning of his life, a period in which he found that he related strongly to the story of a traveler who jumps into a well in the ground, in order to escape a beast that is chasing him, only to find that at the bottom of the well there is a dragon waiting to devour him. As he clings to the branch of a bush in the wall of the well, holding on for dear life so as not to fall toward the dragon, he licks drops of honey and watches two mice, one black and one white, slowly circling and gnawing away at the trunk of the bush. Tolstoy conveys that this story struck him not as a trifling fable but as an indubitable, veritable reflection of the human condition. Sources in which Tolstoy had previously found meaning – in literature, art, science, rational knowledge, family, home, friends, possessions, and professional success – he dismisses as not providing satisfying answers to his questions concerning why he should live. Finally, he recounts looking to the workers in the field who have simple faith in God and who believe that all will be well, writing that he himself found at this point that he had to adopt this mindset, which had seemed to him all along to be irrational and monstrous, in order that he might not take his own life.

As philosophers who examine theoretical reasons, seek evidence, and construct and critique arguments, we might find Tolstoy's professed abandonment of theoretical reason dissatisfying. It is not as if he describes having worked out the arguments from evil, finding a way to make sense of the wrongdoing and suffering in this world before his endorsement of God's existence. He writes with admiration of the simple mindset shared by the laborers, noting that he sees no theoretical rationality in the doctrines of heaven and hell or in the complexities of trinitarian monotheism, yet, nonetheless, he opts to join those who simply believe in God and who accept without questioning the sufferings and afflictions that occur to them and to those around them.

Might Tolstoy's account serve as one way into thinking of belief in God as justified pragmatically? Perhaps one might decide that it is useful to believe in God or that it is good to believe in God for practical reasons. Among these might be the provision of a sense of purpose when one has lost a feeling of fulfillment or the ability to actively engage in projects one had previously taken to have positive value, such as writing works of literature. The thought is, if belief in God helps keep a person from suicide, then perhaps no one should criticize it. It is true that religious faith can give us hope. There is tremendous hope in the thought that there may be a glorious life after our lives on Earth, a heavenly existence in which we experience no pain and no heartbreak, a life in which we enjoy the presence of God, and perhaps other people, forever. Such hope may help us to cope with current pains and injustices in this world, and a religious life might contribute to overall well-being. Notice that the comforts and joys of living in a religious community offering mutual support, and the calming and celebratory rituals offered by religion, provide significant benefits in a world that can be difficult and lonely to navigate and to bear for many people. Are not pragmatic reasons for religious commitment legitimate and worthy of our respect?

One important consideration in this regard is that of harm. In religious commitment and involvement, there is potential for harm to oneself, as well as for harm to others. First, with respect to oneself: we ought to strive to protect the integrity of our intellect together with our practice. That is, actions that are out of accord with what we accept to be true can generate discord in our psyches, which can erode our self-respect. Acting as if something is true that we take to be theoretically not rational to believe endangers the coherence of our self-concept. Second, with respect to others: we should take care in our allegiances and our everyday actions not to play a role in harming other persons. Aligning oneself with a white nationalist organization, for instance, harms others, as does donating to politicians who promote lies about election legitimacy and outcome. In our religious affiliations, including participation in the worship services of a community, we place ourselves as standing with people who affirm particular doctrines, creeds, social practices, and attitudes. We should take care that these practices and attitudes do not cause harm to other persons. I take it that among the potential problematic practices is support for legal and social inequality for adult persons who love and wish to marry another adult person of the same gender or sex, or of a different race or religion. Another is political advocacy against the use of stem cells in medical research, which might help treat disease or paralysis (Sinnott-Armstrong, 2007). Another is behavior toward others that displays condescension concerning their lack of faith and conveys the conviction that they are going to hell. These actions harm people by imposing unjust burdens and causing physical and emotional pain.

In sum, in assessing the matter of the pragmatic justification of religious belief, one would need to take care in what one's religious commitment made for pragmatic reasons led one to do, and the allegiances and attitudes it led one to have, weighing up the costs and benefits while attending to moral considerations.

References

Adams, Marilyn (1986). Redemptive Suffering: A Christian Solution to the Problem of Evil. In Robert Audi and William J. Wainwright, eds., *Rationality, Religious Belief and Moral Commitment*, Ithaca, NY: Cornell University Press, 248–267.

Adams, Marilyn (1989). Horrendous Evils and the Goodness of God, *Proceedings of the Aristotelian Society* 63, 297–310.

Adams, Marilyn (1999). *Horrendous Evils and the Goodness of God*, Ithaca, NY: Cornell University Press.

Alston, William (1991). The Inductive Argument from Evil and the Human Cognitive Condition, *Philosophical Perspectives* 5, 29–67.

Aquinas, Thomas (c. 1270/1920). *Summa Theologica*, revised ed., trans. Fathers of the English Dominican Province, New York: Benzinger Brothers.

Augustine, Saint (c. 426/1950). *The City of God*, trans. Marcus Dods, George Wilson, and J. J. Smith, New York: Random House.

Augustine, Saint (c. 400/1977). *Confessions*, trans. Maria Boulding. Hyde Park, NY: New York City Press.

Bergmann, Michael (2009). Skeptical Theism and the Problem of Evil. In Thomas Flint and Michael Rea, eds., *The Oxford Handbook of Philosophical Theology*, New York: Oxford University Press, 374–399.

Collins, Robin (2013). The Connection-Building Theodicy. In Justin McBrayer and Daniel Howard-Snyder, eds., *The Blackwell Companion to Skeptical Theism*, Malden, MA: Wiley-Blackwell, 222–235.

Dougherty, Trent and Justin McBrayer, eds. (2014). *Skeptical Theism: New Essays*, Oxford: Oxford University Press.

Draper, Paul (1996). The Skeptical Theist. In Daniel Howard-Snyder, ed., *The Evidential Argument from Evil*, Bloomington: Indiana University Press, 175–192.

Ekstrom, Laura (2000). *Free Will: A Philosophical Study*, Boulder, CO: Westview Press.

Ekstrom, Laura (2004). Suffering as Religious Experience. In Peter Van Inwagen, ed., *Christian Faith and the Problem of Evil*, Grand Rapids, MI: Eerdmans, 95–110.

Ekstrom, Laura (2019). Toward a Plausible Event-Causal Indeterminist Account of Free Will, *Synthese* 196 (no. 1), 127–144.

Ekstrom, Laura (2021). *God, Suffering, and the Value of Free Will*, New York: Oxford University Press.

Fischer, John Martin (2012). *Deep Control: Essays on Free Will and Value*, Oxford: Oxford University Press.

Flinders, Carol L. (1993). *Enduring Grace: Living Portraits of Seven Women Mystics*, New York: Harper Collins.

Frankfurt, Harry (1971). Freedom of the Will and the Concept of a Person. *Journal of Philosophy* 68, 5–20.

Frankfurt, Harry (2004). *The Reasons of Love*, Princeton, NJ: Princeton University Press.

Harris, Michael J. (2016). But Now My Eye Has Seen You: Yissurin Shel Ahavah as Divine Intimacy Theodicy, *Torah U-Madda Journal* 17, 64–92.

Hasker, William (1992). The Necessity of Gratuitous Evil. *Faith and Philosophy* 9 (no. 1), 23–44.

Hasker, William (1998). The Foundations of Theism: Scoring the Quinn–Plantinga Debate. *Faith and Philosophy* 15 (no. 1), 52–67.

Hasker, William (2010). All Too Skeptical Theism. *International Journal for Philosophy of Religion* 68, 15–29.

Hick, John (1978). *Evil and the God of Love*, 2nd ed., San Francisco, CA: Harper & Row.

Howard-Snyder, Daniel, ed. (1996). *The Evidential Argument from Evil*, Bloomington: Indiana University Press.

Jordan, Jeff (2004). Divine Love and Human Suffering. *International Journal for Philosophy of Religion* 56, 169–178.

Julian of Norwich (c. 1400/1984). *Revelations of Divine Love*, trans. Elizabeth Spearing, New York: Penguin Books.

Kristof, Nicholas and Sheryl WuDunn (2009). *Half the Sky*, New York: Vintage Books.

Kushner, Harold (1981). *When Bad Things Happen to Good People*, New York: Anchor Books.

Lewis, David (2007). Divine Evil. In Louise Antony, ed., *Philosophers without Gods*, New York: Oxford University Press, 17–31.

Maitzen, Stephen (2009). Ordinary Morality Implies Atheism. *European Journal for Philosophy of Religion* 2, 107–126.

McBrayer, Justin (2013). Counterpart and Appreciation Theodicies. In Justin McBrayer and Daniel Howard-Snyder, eds., *The Blackwell Companion to Skeptical Theism*, Malden, MA: Wiley-Blackwell, 192–204.

McBrayer, Justin and Daniel Howard-Snyder, eds. (2013). *The Blackwell Companion to the Problem of Evil*, Malden, MA: Wiley-Blackwell.

Meister, Chad and Paul Moser, eds. (2017). *The Cambridge Companion to the Problem of Evil*, New York: Cambridge University Press.

Murphy, Mark (2017). *God's Own Ethics: Norms of Divine Agency and the Argument from Evil*, Oxford: Oxford University Press.

Nelkin, Dana (2011). *Making Sense of Freedom and Responsibility*. Oxford: Oxford University Press.

O'Connor, Timothy (forthcoming). Laura Ekstrom's God, Suffering, and the Value of Free Will, *Faith and Philosophy*.

Oppy, Graham (2013). Rowe's Evidential Arguments from Evil. In Justin McBrayer and Daniel Howard-Snyder, eds., *The Blackwell Companion to Skeptical Theism*, Oxford: Wiley-Blackwell, 49–66.

Pereboom, Derk (2013). A Defense without Free Will. In Justin McBrayer and Daniel Howard-Snyder, eds., *The Blackwell Companion to Skeptical Theism*, Oxford: Wiley-Blackwell, 411–425.

Peterson, Michael (2022). *Monotheism, Suffering, and Evil*, Cambridge: Cambridge University Press.

Pew Research Center (2021). Views on the Afterlife, November 23, www.pewresearch.org/religion/2021/11/23/views-on-the-afterlife.

Plantinga, Alvin (1974). *God, Freedom, and Evil*, Grand Rapids, MI: William B. Eerdmans.

Plantinga, Alvin (2000). *Warranted Christian Belief*, New York: Oxford University Press.

Plantinga, Alvin (2004). Supralapsarianism, or "O Felix Culpa." In Peter Van Inwagen, ed., *Christian Faith and the Problem of Evil*, Grand Rapids, MI: William B. Eerdmans, 1–25.

Rea, Michael (2013). The "Too-Much-Skepticism" Objection. In Justin McBrayer and Daniel Howard-Snyder, eds., *The Blackwell Companion to Skeptical Theism*, Oxford: Wiley-Blackwell, 486–506.

Rowe, William (1979). The Problem of Evil and Some Varieties of Atheism. *American Philosophical Quarterly* 16, 335–341.

Rowe, William (1988). Evil and Theodicy. *Philosophical Topics* 16, 119–132.

Rowe, William (1996). The Evidential Argument from Evil: A Second Look. In Daniel Howard-Snyder, ed., *The Evidential Argument from Evil*, Bloomington: Indiana University Press, 262–285.

Senor, Thomas (2013). Skeptical Theism, CORNEA, and Common Sense Epistemology. In Justin McBrayer and Daniel Howard-Snyder, eds., *The Blackwell Companion to Skeptical Theism*, Oxford: Wiley-Blackwell, 426–443.

Sinnott-Armstrong, Walter (2007). Overcoming Christianity. In Louise Antony, ed., *Philosophers without Gods*, New York: Oxford University Press, 69–79.

Speak, Daniel (2015). *The Problem of Evil*, Malden, MA: Polity Press.

Stump, Eleonore (1985). The Problem of Evil, *Faith and Philosophy* 2, 392–423.

Stump, Eleonore (1994). The Mirror of Evil. In Thomas V. Morris, ed., *God and the Philosophers*, New York: Oxford University Press, 235–247.

Stump, Eleonore (1999). *The Stob Lectures*, Grand Rapids, MI: The Stob Lectures Endowment.

Sullivan, Meghan (2013). Peter van Inwagen's Defense. In Justin McBrayer and Daniel Howard-Snyder, eds., *The Blackwell Companion to Skeptical Theism*, Oxford: Wiley-Blackwell, 396–410.

Swinburne, Richard (1998). *Providence and the Problem of Evil*, Oxford: Oxford University Press.

Taylor, Richard (1970). The Meaning of Life. In Richard Taylor, *Good and Evil*, New York: Macmillan.

Tolstoy, Leo (1882/2008). My Confession. In E. D. Klemke and Steven Kahn, eds., *The Meaning of Life: A Reader*, 3rd ed., New York: Oxford University Press, 7–16.

Trakakis, Nick (2013). Antitheodicy. In Justin McBrayer and Daniel Howard-Snyder, eds., *The Blackwell Companion to Skeptical Theism*, Oxford: Wiley-Blackwell, 363–376.

Van Inwagen, Peter (2006). *The Problem of Evil*, Oxford: Clarendon Press.

Watson, Gary (1975). Free Agency. *Journal of Philosophy* 72, 205–220.

Weil, Simone (1951). *Waiting for God*, trans. Emma Craufurd. New York: Harper & Row.

Wolf, Susan (1990). *Freedom within Reason*, Oxford: Oxford University Press.

Wolf, Susan (2007). The Meaning of Lives. In John Perry, Michael Bratman, and John Martin Fischer, eds., *Introduction to Philosophy: Classical and Contemporary Readings*, New York: Oxford University Press, 62–73.

Wolf, Susan (2010). *Meaning in Life and Why It Matters*, Princeton, NJ: Princeton University Press.

Wolterstorff, Nicholas (1987). *Lament for a Son*, Grand Rapids, MI: William B. Eerdmans.

Wolterstorff, Nicholas (1988). Suffering Love. In Thomas V. Morris, ed., *Philosophy and the Christian Faith*, Notre Dame, IN: University of Notre Dame Press.

World Health Organization (2019). Maternal Mortality, September 19, www.who.int/news-room/fact-sheets/detail/maternal-mortality.

Wykstra, Stephen (1984). The Humean Obstacle to Evidential Arguments from Suffering: On Avoiding the Evils of Appearance. *International Journal for Philosophy of Religion* 16, 73–93.

Wykstra, Stephen (1996). Rowe's Noseeum Arguments from Evil. In Daniel Howard-Snyder, ed., *The Evidential Argument from Evil*, Bloomington: Indiana University Press, 126–150.

Cambridge Elements ≡

The Problems of God

Series Editor

Michael L. Peterson
Asbury Theological Seminary

Michael Peterson is Professor of Philosophy at Asbury Theological Seminary. He is the author of *God and Evil* (Routledge); *Monotheism, Suffering, and Evil* (Cambridge University Press); *With All Your Mind* (University of Notre Dame Press); *C. S. Lewis and the Christian Worldview* (Oxford University Press); *Evil and the Christian God* (Baker Book House); and *Philosophy of Education: Issues and Options* (Intervarsity Press). He is co-author of *Reason and Religious Belief* (Oxford University Press); *Science, Evolution, and Religion: A Debate about Atheism and Theism* (Oxford University Press); and *Biology, Religion, and Philosophy* (Cambridge University Press). He is editor of *The Problem of Evil: Selected Readings* (University of Notre Dame Press). He is co-editor of *Philosophy of Religion: Selected Readings* (Oxford University Press) and *Contemporary Debates in Philosophy of Religion* (Wiley-Blackwell). He served as General Editor of the Blackwell monograph series Exploring Philosophy of Religion and is founding Managing Editor of the journal *Faith and Philosophy*.

About the Series

This series explores problems related to God, such as the human quest for God or gods, contemplation of God, and critique and rejection of God. Concise, authoritative volumes in this series will reflect the methods of a variety of disciplines, including philosophy of religion, theology, religious studies, and sociology.

Cambridge Elements ☰

The Problems of God

Elements in the Series

Divine Guidance: Moral Attraction in Action
Paul K. Moser

God, Salvation, and the Problem of Spacetime
Emily Qureshi-Hurst

Orthodoxy and Heresy
Steven Nemes

God and Political Theory
Tyler Dalton McNabb

Evolution and Christianity
Michael Ruse

Evil and Theodicy
Laura W. Ekstrom

A full series listing is available at: www.cambridge.org/EPOG

Printed in the United States
by Baker & Taylor Publisher Services